Home Education in INDIANA 2016

Indiana Association of Home Educators {IA

P.O. Box 217

Stilesville, IN 46180

317.467.6244

info@iahe.net

www.iahe.net

Dedicated to the servant leaders of the IAHE who have given countless hours to Encourage, Protect, and Serve Indiana homeschool families since 1983.

But they who wait for the Lord shall renew their strength; they shall mount up with wings like eagles; they shall run and not be weary; they shall walk and not faint.

Isaiah 40:31

Home Education in Indiana compiled by the IAHE

© 2000, 2007, & 2016

Thank you to the many authors who have allowed their words of wisdom to be shared and reprinted. Thank you to Breezy Brookshire (breezytulip.com) for the use of her illustration "Teach Them Diligently". Thank you to project editors Jennifer Mayhill, Theresa Slinkard, Kelsi Hirschy, Amanda Alexander, and Cassie Bottorff. Thank you to Melinda Martin (melindamartin.me) for her dedication, patience, sense of humor, and publishing & design skills.

10 Ways to CONNECT TO THE IAHE

 Website & Blog

 Meet Your Rep

 enewsletter

 IAHE Convention

 Facebook

 Facebook Discussion Group

 Google+

 Twitter

 Pinterest

 Instagram

Indiana Association of Home Educators

Table of Contents

The Indiana Association of Home Educators {IAHE}
is here to help provide answers.

The IAHE is a not-for-profit organization founded in 1983 to support and
encourage families interested in home education.

The IAHE is a Christian organization that serves all homeschool families.

We define home education as
parent-directed, home-based, privately-funded education.

Introduction - Where Do I Start?

Tara Bentley | Executive Director

Since 1983, the IAHE has helped thousands of Indiana families begin their homeschool journey. For many years we published *Home Education in Indiana* to help answer the most frequently asked questions from new families.

While a lot has changed in the homeschooling world over the past thirty-plus years, this opening sentence from the last edition of *Home Education in Indiana* rings just as true today as it did in the past.

> *At the IAHE Office, the most frequently asked question is "Where do I start?"*

In the information age it might seem that the answer to this question is an easy one in 2016.

The truth is that today more than ever, families are making the decision to homeschool, and many find themselves overwhelmed with the vast number of options and choices before them.

The time was right to bring *Home Education in Indiana* back! This book is just a short introduction to home education. It is designed to give you the confidence to begin homeschooling, and to provide you with a greater understanding of the concept of home education. This 2016 revision of our book is a mix of classic articles from the IAHE Archives along with fresh content to help you along the way.

> *The mention of homeschooling brings varied pictures to people's minds. Some people imagine a small schoolroom with desks, books, and an American flag. Others picture a mother sitting on the couch or at the kitchen table surrounded by children and textbooks. Still others think of a less formal setting of children at the park, or the museum, or in the garage working on a carpentry project.*

> *These pictures are all accurate. There are probably as many different styles of homeschools as there are families that homeschool. Home education simply means that the parents are responsible for their children's entire education. Part of this education may be delegated to another individual, such as a tutor, music teacher, coach, etc., but ultimately the parent controls and chooses the method of education.*

> *It is the hope of the IAHE that the information will help you to make wise choices for your family. We have not attempted to cover in depth the broad subject of home education, but only those questions that apply specifically to Indiana. Many excellent books on home education are currently available. Consider obtaining one of these books or checking out the homeschool section of your library. We hope the information provided is helpful to you. We are here to serve you and to answer any additional questions that may arise.*

what is the IAHE?

Indiana Association of Home Educators:
Yesterday and Today

In January of 1983, a small group of Christian home educators recognized the need to provide support for the growing number of Hoosier homeschooling families. Three couples gathered around a kitchen table to discuss home education. As the word spread, more families came to the monthly meetings. Their first event was a workshop on character building with Ron & Rebekah Coriell. Shortly after, they sponsored a Gregg Harris "Homeschooling Workshop" in the War Memorial auditorium in downtown Indianapolis. Outgrowing the facility, the first annual homeschool convention was held at Heritage Christian School in Indianapolis in 1985. Four hundred parents attended. With each passing year the convention grew.

Originally, the only help the three couples had was one grandmother who volunteered to do all the secretarial work and bookkeeping in her bedroom. In 1992, office space was rented for the grandmother when her room became too full. A paid staff was hired in 1994.

In 2001, the IAHE had two paid staff, a volunteer Board of Directors, and 16 geographically located volunteer couples, called Regional Representatives. In 2007 the organization began to feel the impact of decreased revenue as a result of the competition from a for-profit convention. As a cost saving measure the Board of Directors made the difficult decision to close the office and let go of the paid staff in 2010. The IAHE survived as an all-volunteer organization with the Board taking on the workload of the organization.

The last few years have seen the resurgence of the IAHE as a strong and healthy organization rising to meet the challenges of a new homeschool community. 2015 saw the IAHE team grow to include a new paid Executive Director, a Lead Regional Representative couple and a Facebook Representative.

Foundational Purpose

The foundational purpose of the IAHE is to serve the Lord Jesus Christ by supporting and encouraging Indiana's home educators. This is accomplished by sponsoring a yearly convention, maintaining visibility with civil government leaders, protecting the parents' rights to homeschool, and publishing additional resources for homeschooling families.

Published quarterly, *The Informer* is an informative magazine, which had a peak circulation of 17,000. Realizing that all Hoosier home educators should have access to this publication, the association took a step of faith to send *The Informer,* free of charge, to all who subscribe. The Lord has provided the funding through advertisements and donations from readers.

The IAHE also strives to influence the legislative process and promotes home education through media relations. A great opportunity to meet the legislators is Home School Day at the Capitol, scheduled each year during the Indiana General Assembly.

Held in Indianapolis, the IAHE's Annual Home Educators' Convention is the primary source of the IAHE's financial revenue. Provided at the convention are well-known speakers and many informative workshops. A huge exhibit hall offers scores of curricula and supplemental materials from which to choose.

Foundational Goals

1. *Maintaining visibility as home educators with civil government leaders*

2. *Influencing the legislative process*

3. *Sponsoring seminars for parent education*

Regional Representatives

The state is divided into 16 regions, each with a Regional Representative couple. One of their responsibilities is to contact the support groups about legislation pertinent to homeschoolers on both the state and national levels.

Other duties of Regional Representatives include helping new homeschoolers find support groups, informing support groups of opportunities and IAHE events, and publicizing the convention. They fulfill several responsibilities at the convention and help at other IAHE events. They also speak at various community events about home education.

IAHE Action

In October of 2015 the IAHE announced the formation of a new sister organization, a 501(c)4 organization, Indiana Association of Home Educators Action. The addition of a 501(c)4 organization will increase the ability and capacity to protect homeschool freedom for future generations.

The mission of Indiana Association of Home Educators Action is to protect Hoosier home education freedom and parental rights by influencing the legislative process. We encourage Indiana home educators to stay vigilant in order to maintain the freedom that has been gained over the years. We do not take our freedom for granted. IAHE Action understands that freedom must be guarded for the benefit of current and future home educating families.

Why the IAHE?

Debi Ketron, IAHE Government Affairs Director

Have you ever wondered why Indiana homeschoolers need a state organization? Years ago homeschoolers were few and far between, curriculum resources were less abundant, and connecting with other like-minded families was difficult. In those days, state homeschool organizations were the hub of all things homeschooling. Today, homeschoolers are much easier to find, curriculum vendors seem to pop up everywhere, and many networking opportunities exist, making the need for a state organization seem less obvious. This may feel especially true here in Indiana, a state where homeschooling is less regulated in comparison to many other states.

The freedom to educate our children at home is a blessing and a constitutional right. Did you know this right is something the IAHE has actively fought to protect for over thirty years? The board members of the IAHE and countless volunteers have worked faithfully behind the scenes in big and little ways to provide many "hidden" benefits to homeschoolers across the state.

The Indiana Association of Home Educators (IAHE) was founded by Judge Ken and Joyce Johnson in 1983, the same year as the *Homeschool Legal Defense Association (HSLDA)*, making it one of the earliest state home education organizations in the nation. The IAHE has been influencing the legislature on behalf of home educators since its inception. When bills are discovered that have the potential to negatively affect homeschool rights, the IAHE contacts HSLDA for their legal opinion. If the proposed legislation has the potential to negatively affect our home educators' freedoms, IAHE leaders head to the State House and work to prevent it from becoming law. **Your homeschooling rights have been protected by the IAHE in numerous sessions of the state legislature.**

The IAHE board also works closely with national organizations to stay informed about issues that homeschooling families in other states are facing in an effort to avoid those challenges here at home. IAHE also works with Dr. Brian Ray of the *National Home Education Research Institute (NHERI)*. As a member of the *National Alliance of Christian Home Education Leadership*, the IAHE networks with other state leaders in the home education movement. These types of relationships provide mutual encouragement, idea sharing, and benefits to homeschooling families statewide.

To more effectively reach local communities, the IAHE provides a volunteer network of Regional Representative couples located in sixteen regions across the state. Along with the board members, these Representatives answer emails, field calls, and counsel individuals in their regions regarding home education. They work to connect and encourage families, and assist in founding new support groups if there is a need. They also assist at the IAHE state convention and speak at local events. If you haven't met your Reps, please use the map and listing on page five and introduce yourself.

Perhaps the most well-known function of the IAHE is its annual Home Educators' Convention with nationally recognized speakers and a large vendor hall. This is a great time of fellowship, encouragement, learning, and exploration for new and veteran parents. Many moms and dads count this weekend as a special time to focus on the Lord's calling to train and disciple their children. Convention proceeds sustain the year-round efforts of the IAHE and help fund community-building events for homeschooling families. Proceeds also support *The Informer* magazine and help home education related entities such as the *Home School Foundation* and the *NHERI*.

Families can connect with the IAHE online in multiple way. Home educators can register on our website to receive up-to-date information on proposed legislation, homeschooling events, and more. A calendar of events for the state is provided on the website and a public forum to ask questions and share information. Homeschoolers can also get connected with the IAHE through Facebook, Instagram, Pinterest, and more. It is easier than ever to stay connected and contribute to the Indiana homeschooling community.

Today's homeschool families have more choices and opportunities than ever before. State organizations play a vital role in helping families navigate choices and make connections, while supporting the very foundations of our legal right to homeschool. In Indiana, the IAHE continues to work hard on your behalf in these areas. With so many areas of impact, today, more than ever, state organizations are needed to encourage, protect, and support you as you home educate your children.

Debi Ketron is wife to Phil and mother to four children. The Ketrons home educated for twenty-one years graduating all of their children from their home school. They served as IAHE Region 8 Representatives before joining the Board of Directors. Phil and Debi reside in Dearborn County.

Freedom Isn't Free

Judge Kenneth Johnson, IAHE Founding Board of Directors Member

IAHE 30th Anniversary Founder Address

Editor's note: In celebration of the 30th anniversary of the IAHE, former board members were invited to attend the annual Home Educators' Convention. The follow is an adaptation of the remarks delivered by one of the IAHE founders, Judge Kenneth Johnson.

It's sometimes hard to imagine that it has been 30 years since the IAHE was born. As one of the founders of the IAHE, my only claim to fame is that we were privileged to be used by God to accomplish His purpose. The three original founding couples—Mark and Ellen Bell, Doug and Nancy Jesch, and Joyce and I—each came to the decision to homeschool our children in quite unique and different ways. Joyce and I first heard about homeschooling while we were attending a legislative conference where the agenda was how to draft a Godly law and how to enforce it. It was there that we met several families that were home educating. We were impressed with their exuberance, their knowledge of their children, and their plans for raising them up, as scripture says, in the way in which they should go.

I don't want it to seem that our decision to homeschool was like a burning bush experience where we clearly saw God's plan for our family. I think you could call our first response, at best, hesitant. As a matter of fact, we even had a back-up plan to make sure that we wouldn't be ruining our oldest child's chances for a Harvard scholarship—even though he was only 5 years old at the time.

When I consider all the details that it took to begin the IAHE, I am overwhelmed at the power of God's hand in it. By happenstance, our three families discovered each other's decision to homeschool our children. We decided to start getting together monthly to share ideas and encouragement. Other couples began joining us in the Bell's basement when word got out about what we were doing. Around that time, Mark and I found ourselves alone together; two fairly new Rambo-like attorneys with a passion. We felt we ought to do something worthwhile with our time, and voila! The corporate charter and bylaws of the IAHE were born.

I can vividly remember those first monthly meetings. We had no money to send out notices nor buy needed supplies, so each meeting began by passing around a microwavable dish to collect donations. Being of a keen judicial mind, I started going to the restroom at the beginning of each meeting, having forgotten that the Jesches and Bells could count and notice my lack of participation.

We soon started getting phone calls from parents who had been visited by a social worker or truant officer, and had been threatened with legal proceedings that would include fines, possible jail time, and the loss of custody of their children. We then got a call from Steve Goldsmith, who was the Marion county prosecutor and was pro-homeschooling. Together, we worked out a set of lenient prosecutorial guidelines. If someone were to visit a homeschooling family and they reported they were home educating their children, they were to be left alone. Mr. Goldsmith sensed that homeschooling families needed protection throughout the state and he sent these guidelines to all 92 county prosecutors with a strong suggestion that they be followed.

I ask you, who could have accomplished this but a loving and awesome God?

Some families were being contacted by the Indiana State Department of Education. It so happened that Sue Ellen Reed, a Hanover college graduate like Mr. Bell and myself, was the superintendent. She was not only convinced that home education was a good thing, she even assigned a person on her staff to assist and protect us. We enjoyed such a positive relationship with the Department of Education that if a parent would contact them about homeschooling, they referred them to us.

I ask you, who could have accomplished this but a loving and awesome God?

We were parents devoting our time to teaching and training our children, and as homeschooling in Indiana grew, we needed someone who could advocate for us in the legislature. Along came a man named Eric Miller. Due to his incredible energy and enthusiasm and his Advance American organization, he became our full-time eyes and ears in the state legislature. When any proposed bill would have an impact on our freedom to homeschool, he would advocate on our behalf and help us organize a response to our legislators.

I ask you, who could have accomplished this but a loving and awesome God?

Next we were introduced to a pastor, teacher, and homeschooling father, Gregg Harris, who became a regular at our early conferences. Gregg also taught an all-day seminar that the IAHE co-sponsored which encouraged, exhorted and taught us how to live and how to train up our children in the way in which they should go.

I ask you, who could have accomplished this but a loving and awesome God?

We discovered that one piece of the puzzle was still missing, especially as we had families being legally challenged. We needed credibility in the academic and educational community. It seemed that the professional educators had 'this' study and 'that' study to prove their success, but we had no one on our side. Along came a statistician, an analyst, and a homeschooling father who filled that need. Brian Ray undertook numerous studies demonstrating the effectiveness of homeschooling, not only as an academic endeavor but as a life enriching experience. Brian continues to be our beacon for shedding light on the blessings and achievements of home educated children and continues to make himself available to testify in court in defense of home education.

I ask you, who could have accomplished this but a loving and awesome God?

If you have not heard a word I have shared thus far – hear this:

The cost of our freedom to choose to teach our children at home, and in our own way, is eternal vigilance. The early goal of the IAHE and HSLDA was to make homeschooling legal in Indiana and in every state. God has given us precious victories in achieving these goals and the worst thing we could do now is to think the fight is over. Please believe me when I tell you it is not. Our freedom to homeschool is always at risk – always!

The legal landscape can change in a heartbeat. It may be in a bill that directly outlaws homeschooling, or a single sentence hidden in a multi-paged bill that escapes notice, or it could be in some obscure administrative rule that denies or hinders your freedom to make the best choices for your family.

I hear people asking, if homeschooling is legal in Indiana and all 50 states, why do I need to support organizations like the IAHE or HSLDA? The answer is simple... because ***freedom isn't free.***

If you want to continue to enjoy the freedoms many others before you have worked and fought for, then be involved. If you want to be encouraged in your homeschool endeavors, to be supported and lifted up, then join with us. If you sense the need for us all to stand firm and united against the worldly forces that would seek to disarm and hinder us, then become an integral part of the solution. Stand with us.

Stand with the IAHE

Tara Bentley, Executive Director

With minimal government regulation, Indiana is one of the best states in the country to homeschool your children. The Indiana Association of Home Educators (IAHE) has been working to maintain the freedom to home educate for over 30 years.

Each year, the IAHE hosts a statewide homeschool convention. They also publish a free quarterly magazine for Indiana families, *The Informer*.

What Else Does the IAHE Do?

The IAHE is a full-time, year-round ministry with a lot of action that goes on behind the scenes. Perhaps you talked with one of our 16 Regional Reps when you began homeschooling. Through our reps, the IAHE connects families with local support groups and help to answer questions. We are often asked to provide help to families that are struggling with the process of withdrawing their student from the public school system. Frequently, families are given misinformation from school personnel regarding Indiana's law on home education. We provide clear answers on what is required.

The IAHE monitors an average of 1,600-2,000 bills each year and targets the ones that may affect homeschool freedom. We monitor the State Board of Education and Indiana's legislative committees, and watch for bills that impact parental rights and more. IAHE follows these bills through the process and watches for amendments. We also meet with state officials to give them a homeschool perspective, and when necessary, send out Action Items to our Indiana families. The IAHE is your homeschool voice in the statehouse.

IAHE was one of the earliest groups in the country to take a position against Common Core in Indiana in January 2012. We have worked to educate the state about the dangers inherent in nationalized education standards. We were sought out and recognized nationally as one of the key organizations in the opposition movement in Indiana.

Occasionally homeschooling receives negative attention in the media. We conduct media interviews throughout the year to ensure that the public understands what true homeschooling looks like. We were also present at the 6th Circuit Court of Appeals in Cincinnati in support of HSLDA and the Romeike family. For 30 years, we've held annual events at the state capitol to bring legislators and homeschoolers together.

In spite of home education proving to be very successful over the years, the challenges to our freedoms have only grown. Indiana is not a homeschool friendly state by chance... we have the freedom to homeschool our children because Indiana families and IAHE leaders have been vigilant for decades.

Each year, we see an increase in the attempts to legislate families. Occasionally, we are called upon to testify before House or Senate committees regarding proposed legislation. Our organization's visibility at the state house, our attendance numbers at the convention, and our subscriber lists, are each critical and vital pieces that make sure that your voice is heard. There is strength in unity. The more Indiana homeschool families stand together, the louder our voices will be heard.

How Can You Help?

- Your convention attendance matters. The IAHE convention is a vital way to showcase our community to the public. Each year, Indiana state legislators are invited to attend the IAHE's Home Educators' Convention. The size of our convention is one way the IAHE is able to demonstrate to legislators the strength of our homeschool community. Your convention registration and your family's presence impact our ability to advocate for you all year long.

- Volunteer. We depend on volunteers to accomplish our mission as we work to protect homeschool families. If you have a servant heart, visit our website for details.

- Donate. Just like all non-profit ministries, we depend on the donations of our supporters. We accept donations year round from individuals and corporate sponsors.

Will You Stand with Us?

Attend. Volunteer. Donate.

And Share.

Your support enables us to protect the freedom to home educate for future generations. Share information about the IAHE on your Facebook page, Pinterest, and more. Talk to your friends and local support group about why Indiana needs a strong state organization. **Stand With Us** and let others know that you support the IAHE's mission to *Encourage, Protect, and Serve* Indiana families interested in home education. When you share about the IAHE, you become an important part of our team.

Tara Bentley is the mother of two beautiful homeschool graduates. When they decided to homeschool in the spring of 2001, they were only considering it as a two year plan. They very quickly realized that the decision to homeschool was one of the best things they could have ever done for their family and their was no going back. Mark and Tara have volunteered with the IAHE since 2011, joined the Board of Directors in 2013, and Tara became the Executive Director in the fall of 2015. They feel blessed to work with the IAHE serving the homeschooling community and protecting homeschool freedom for the next generation.

IAHE Regions

As a means of connecting new homeschoolers to the support needed, the IAHE has selected 16 experienced homeschool couples as Regional Representatives. Each Representative is a 'veteran' homeschooler who can answer questions from families starting their homeschooling years. Regional Representatives also communicate with the local support groups in their region and keep them up to date on changes in the law and activities throughout the state. A current list of Regional Representatives appears in each issue of *The Informer* magazine and can also be found on our website: iahe.net.

Deciding to Homeschool

Why Home Education?

Home education is a serious commitment for any family. Knowing why you have chosen home education for your children is important because: it will guide you in the proper selection of educational materials; it will prepare you with a solid answer when someone questions your decision to home educate; it will enable your children to see and appreciate the commitment you have made in the decision to home educate; and it will provide you with the determination and motivation to keep going when you have doubts or experience difficulties. Therefore it would be wise to develop an "educational philosophy" in which you define your reasons for choosing home education.

In developing this philosophy, you may want to consider the following questions:

- What do I believe about my relationship with God?
- Who is responsible for the training (education) of my children?
- What is my definition of successful education?
- What are my academic goals, and how do I want to achieve them?
- What values do I believe need to be imparted to my children?

It is strongly suggested that you research, study, and prayerfully consider this undertaking before deciding that home education is the right choice for your family.

Deciding to Homeschool

Teaching your children is a God-given responsibility, which qualifies you to home educate your children. God commands all parents to teach their children His Word, the most important thing they will ever learn. Since you know your children better than anyone else, you are able to meet their needs better than anyone else. Your love and the desire you have to ensure that your children will receive a quality education are your greatest assets. You don't have to know everything before you begin. Your example and enthusiasm will motivate and encourage your children as you learn with them.

"And you shalt love the Lord thy God with all thine heart and with all thy soul and with all thy might. And these words, which I command thee this day, shall be in thine heart; and thou shalt teach them diligently unto thy children, and thou shalt talk of them when thou sittest in thine house, and when thou walkest by the way, and when thou liest down, and when thou riseth up."

Deuteronomy 6:5-7

What is Homeschooling?

Definitions Matter

Does it matter that the term "homeschooling" is used by those who are not homeschooling in the traditional manner?

Occasionally the IAHE sees conversations in social media that mention other forms of education where the term "homeschooling" is used. It is not anyone's goal to demean a different option; but, often concerned individuals become very passionate in their discussions when pointing out that there is a difference. IAHE has made a point of defining homeschooling as **parent-directed, home-based, and privately-funded education**. Research has shown that thoughtful parental engagement ***with their own children*** has proven to have lasting, positive effects. This is the type of education that the IAHE has been promoting since 1983 and legislators know it is effective.

*Why does it matter that others who are **not** promoting this type of education are also using the term "homeschooling"?*

Indiana Code classifies a homeschool as a non-accredited, nonpublic school. With all of the educational options that fall under that category, it is important that we clarify the definition of homeschool and home education. It is critical for families to understand that virtual charter public schools do not fall under this category at all. Even though the school work is being done at home, these growing virtual school options are legally defined as accredited, public schools.

It is imperative that we do not lose the definition of homeschooling.

With all the school choice alternatives, the water is becoming very muddy. With unclear definitions come confusion and increased chance of regulation. **IAHE has watched as other states have seen attempts to increase regulation due this confusion, and IAHE is trying to protect the movement in Indiana.**

Invite your friends to join us on Facebook in the IAHE Homeschool Discussion group; the more Indiana homeschoolers understand the importance of this, the easier it will be to protect our freedom. Standing together, we can protect our cherished freedom in Indiana and provide the best education available to our children. **Parent-directed, home-based, privately-funded education is a proven method for providing an excellent education.**

Homeschooling works; don't settle for anything less!

More Homeschool Definitions

Support Group: A group of homeschool families who interact on a regular basis for the purpose of networking, sharing resources, providing opportunities for socialization (for each other and/or their children.) Sometimes support groups are primarily co-ops or have co-ops that exist within them.

Co-op: A homeschool co-op can be a very casual group of moms getting together to do a class or activity together or a more formal setup with designated teachers, classes, fees, etc. A co-op, in its truest form, is a meeting that focuses on learning where all the parents take turns teaching all subjects to all of the children. However, in truth, co-ops are as different as the people who set them up and run them. Teachers can be parents who volunteer or people (parents or nonparents) with specific knowledge in an academic area who are paid. Often formal co-ops have some kind of board or leadership structure and a set of by-laws.

Cottage School: A cottage school is run by paid teachers. It may be as simple as one teacher with one child or it may be a more formal version of the co-op. They may offer fun, elective type classes or academic classes that provide the full curriculum which the parents must continue at home. Many of them work on a University Model. This model is characterized by operating with a "drop-off" mentality for parents, classes that often meet more than once a week, and curriculum choices are dictated by the school and not the parents.

What About Virtual School Options?

K12, Connections Academy, and several other virtual schools are popular, school-at-home, public school options for many families. But by definition, they are still **_public school_** options. Therefore they operate and are subject to different laws and guidelines as homeschools (nonpublic, non-accredited). Often the primary instruction is via classes on the internet. Material may be provided at low or no cost to the parents, including textbooks and computers, but the student is legally a _public_ student not a homeschool student even when they are doing these classes at home. It is important to distinguish the difference between homeschooling and a public school-at-home program because the government, through your tax dollars, funds these programs and participants must follow any program mandates or requirements presented by the public school system. Because these programs are government funded, faith-based curriculum is often not allowed. These public school-at-home programs work for many families and you should do what works best for your students.

A Cautionary Tale

We LOVE homeschooling.

We believe it is the best choice for our children.

We believe that parents should be informed about the negative trends, issues and ideology in the public school system today.

We value parental rights and homeschool freedom, and all of the benefits that come with it.

And we believe in fighting to defend those freedoms.

Sometimes that love and the fight for freedom can result in heated conversations, lax attitudes, and prideful comments. And in spite of our very best intentions as a community, we find ourselves in a dangerous waters when we aren't careful.

Caution #1

Our love of homeschooling should not be expressed at the expense of others. The public schools are filled with some pretty ugly stuff that we do not want our children exposed to. But they are also filled with countless, loving and dedicated teachers and professionals who work hard each day to make a difference. We should be careful to not present over-reaching generalizations and arguments that depict all public school personnel negatively.

Caution #2

Our freedom to homeschool can not be taken for granted or abused. Yes, you can and should modify your student's educational experience to meet their needs. No, you should not give high school credit for classes without true academic achievement. Integrity matters! Issuing a high school diploma without true educational merit threatens homeschool freedom for generations to come.

Caution #3

Our pride in our children and in the homeschooling community should not be confused with an air of perfection. Yes, we believe that homeschooling is the best choice for us. No, we do not believe that it is the ONLY choice. Homeschooling isn't easy and no one does it without making mistakes. Many families are not in the position to homeschool. Others are just not called to homeschool. Pride is a dangerous attitude that keeps us from seeing our own flaws.

We LOVE homeschooling, homeschool parents, homeschool families and graduates!

But we must be careful in our words and deeds that we do not allow this love to become an idol and a hindrance in our conversations with others.

Home Education Works

Indiana is a great state in which to home educate students. Home educating families appreciate the freedoms and flexibility that homeschooling offers. Learning together, families love the special bond that is created within the home. Home education in Indiana gives students an excellent knowledge of academic subjects and prepares children to be extraordinary adults.

Indiana Law States:

1. *The Indiana homeschool is considered a non-accredited private school.*

2. *Beginning in the fall of the school year in which the child turns seven (or earlier if enrolled in your private school) until the child turns 18 or graduates, your child must attend school for the same number of days public schools are in session. Generally, that is 180 days each year.*

3. *Attendance records must be kept and may be requested by the state superintendent or the local public school superintendent to verify attendance. Therefore it is*

recommended that you keep your attendance record separate from your weekly lesson plans.

4. *The child is to be taught in the English language.*

5. *A private school administrator shall furnish upon request of the state superintendent of public instruction, the number of children by grade level attending the school. This request should be an individual request and not a blanket announcement such as the one on the Indiana Department of Education's website to the public at large. Please understand that this is not a registration form or a request to homeschool but it's a form to report that you have a private school with students enrolled in your school.*

6. *The child must be provided with instruction equivalent to that given in public schools, but the State Board of Education is not given the authority to define "equivalent instruction" nor to approve of homeschools. In fact the law has removed all subject requirements, leaving homeschools without any mandatory subjects.*

Home education takes commitment.

Please pray and research home education before you withdraw your children from the traditional school or begin to school at home. Talk to other home educators, learn the state law, read books on the topic of homeschooling, and shop for curriculum. Please seek God's wisdom and educate yourself **before** you decide to home educate.

Home education takes money to purchase school curriculum and supplies, and to cover activity fees. The amount spent per child varies and depends on the curriculum choices of an individual family. More money will be spent if parents desire that the curriculum do more of the teaching and planning; less money if parents are willing to give more of their time to prep and teach each subject.

Home education takes time.

Although students must be educated the same number of days as the public schools, each private school may choose the days and times that their school will be in session and record it on their school's attendance record. Usually the bookwork in the early grades can be done in 1-2 hours per day, but as the child grows older it takes more time, about 4-5 hours a day. It is important that parents consider the time required to educating their children.

Should you decide to home educate, discussing with your spouse what your approach to homeschooling will be is the next thing to do before purchasing curriculum and starting your school year. Make a list of why you both wish to home educate and what goals you would like your children to achieve this year and in the years to follow. Not only will this list include the basic academic objectives but it should also include character goals and basic life skills, such as budgeting and maintaining the house and cars.

Sometimes home educators get discouraged and lose track of their goals; therefore having a vision will help to keep your family going in the day-to-day tasks of what is required. As new home educators, it may seem easy to read many how-to homeschooling books and then become overwhelmed by the variety of advice offered in the books, but don't allow them to overwhelm you. Spending time around other people who share your vision can keep homeschooling enjoyably fresh. Participating in a few field trips or a co-op class with several home educating families can strengthen both your family and the others. It can be very easy to get bogged down with too many details and forget the reason you have chosen to home educate in the first place. Make your lists. Have a plan. Connect with other home educators through your local support group. Thinking through your approach to homeschooling will benefit your family throughout the years to come.

Are you ready to begin a wonderful family experience? Then discuss home education with your spouse, order your materials, and get started. Enjoy your children. Enjoy the experience. Enjoy the fact that home education does work!

The Importance of Developing Your Written Philosophy of Education

Penny Taylor, M.Ed. | IAHE Board Member

The benefit of having a road map to get to your destination without getting lost is commonly understood. With that plan in hand, even if you get confused, you are able to find your way back to the right road. A written philosophy of education is much the same thing for your homeschooling journey.

Before all the planning for school supplies, curricula, and field trips, take some time to think through what you believe about education. What's its purpose? What's its goal? What's *your* goal in homeschooling? If you've decided not to entrust the academic part of your children's training to anyone else, you really should think about it. If you're relying on the curriculum to just do it for you, you need to remember that curriculum – any curriculum – is simply a tool. What do you intend to accomplish with the tool in your hand?

Think about how your children learn. You know what makes things "click" for them. How do they learn? What modality is their strongest learning style - are they kinesthetic learners, visual learners, or aural learners? What's their weakest one? You've been their teacher since they were born so you know them better than anyone. "Academics" is simply a part of your overall teaching, training, and mentoring of your children.

Ultimately, what you think about their education will determine both your methodology and the tools you choose. Certainly consider your children's learning styles but remember that any tool you use should fit you, too. So, take a good look at how *you* teach – that's your teaching style. What tools (curricula) are most comfortable for you to use? Most of us have gone through an educational system that is Greek in its origin: a classroom setting with a teacher at the front of the room, imparting information. Homeschooling is a more relaxed, natural, relationship-based, one-on-one tutorial model with a touch of the one-room schoolhouse, teaching to the bent of the child. Maybe you need to reconsider your approach. As a former public school teacher, I did.

It has been said that you really don't know what you think until you write it down. So, spending some time coming up with – and writing down – your philosophy of education is certainly not wasted time. To the contrary, it's actually quite productive, saving both time and money as you sift through the plethora of ideas and approaches that will come your way, allowing you to blow away the chaff and keep the grain. More importantly, if you will remember to read it, it will get you back on the path … your own words of wisdom will encourage you when the vision begins to dim and you think you can't go on or that you're messing up your children.

Many years ago, I wrote out our philosophy of education, a rather impassioned piece penned after thinking and praying about our children, our family, and the uncertain future at which our arrows were aimed. It centered on the reason why we were doing what we were doing. In the years that followed, I brought out that document many times, even some years putting it under the see-through front cover of my planning binder so that I'd see it every day. It's helped keep me focused, allowing me to remind myself – yea, counsel myself – in times of burnout and trial as I revisited the reasons that readied and steadied me for yet another day. Having put my hand to the plow, I didn't want to look back; we, who plow, plow in hope. I wanted to do my best and trust the results to the Lord.

So, if you are new to the idea of homeschooling, how do you get started thinking about something you've never thought of before? Or how do you fine-tune in practical ways the broad thoughts you've had about education? How do you work out that philosophy in your daily homeschooling? Start with the reasons you investigated homeschooling in the first place. What brought you to this point? Then, read and listen to others who are knowledgeable on the subject. Discover the basics taught by early homeschooling pioneers such as Dr. Raymond, Dorothy Moore, and Dr. Ruth Beechick and then add to that those who have come after them. Listen to homeschooling speakers – in person or recordings – at your state convention; that's your continuing education and so important to your on-going task, no matter where you are in your homeschooling journey.

Education for the homeschooler is much broader than the rather limited definition of academic success in our culture. It is so very much more overarching and all-encompassing. In Webster's 1828 Dictionary, "education" is defined as "the bringing up, as of a child, instruction; formation of manners. Education comprehends all that series of instruction and discipline which is intended to enlighten the understanding, correct the temper, and form the manners and habits of youth, and fit them for usefulness in their future stations. To give children a good education in manners, arts and science, is important; to give them a religious education is indispensable; and an immense responsibility rests on parents and guardians who neglect these duties." [1] Ponder the scope of that definition.

Figure out a way to fold learning into your family as a way of life, not a separate compartment in a box called "School at Home." Seek to make your children life-long learners as you learn together, not with just the goal of getting through high school and into college. Consider that your children will need to develop both a love of learning and the skills of how to learn because, as we know, in this Information Age, information changes as fast as you can learn it. Help them learn the basics, with the added tool of research; encourage curiosity, creativity, and play; read to them throughout the years; teach them to work; and aim at a target - follow whatever plan you choose. All along the way, develop their character through responsibility – something paramount to employers who are willing to train skills but know they can't train character. All of this is accomplished not merely with a curriculum, computer, or co-op classes - it requires you.

Inevitably, you will have opportunities – and perhaps some pressure – to join co-ops and on-line classes. While it's not wrong to take advantage of a certain class or course of study that these opportunities may afford, think carefully about how much of your precious teaching time you will hand-off to others. Be judicious and selective. Instead of fleeing to co-ops because you don't think you can do it, consider learning *with* your children. Part of the mentoring of homeschooling is learning together and having your children experience your enthusiasm... and even your struggle, trumped by a greater determination to succeed. It's easier today than ever before to access to the things we don't know or understand. Don't forget to seek support from some homeschooling moms who've "been there." You CAN do this.

These years are precious. One day your homeschooling journey will be behind you and you will have done it one way or the other, with memories, regrets, successes, and maybe some failures – and all of it will be used. So be intentional. You will soon see just how fleeting those teachable moments are. Today, there exists the lure to return in some degree to the public school for sports and other curricular and extracurricular activities or to enroll your child in either private schools or in those co-ops run as schools. Don't take the bait. The years with your children in your home really are very few. You will never regret the time you invested in their lives while you had the opportunity. Be purposeful. Regret is a haunting thing; decide not to allow the ground for its growth. Spend time with your children and invest in their future. One day, you'll have some great stories to tell your grandchildren.

Penny Taylor, married to Steve for forty years, is the mother of nine. They have homeschooled all of their children, now ages 18 to adult. With four daughters married, they are the grandparents of 14 homeschooled –and future homeschooled – grandchildren. A former public school teacher, she still holds an Indiana teaching license. Steve and Penny live on a small farm in rural west central Indiana and currently serve on the Board of the IAHE.

Indiana Homeschool Laws

Families considering homeschooling for the first time may find themselves overwhelmed. Our goal is to encourage you along the way and provide you with valuable helps and resources that will help you make the best decision for your family.

Indiana Law

We are not attorneys, so the IAHE does NOT give legal advice. The content in this book is provided for informational purposes only. Regulations may change at any time and it is vital for homeschool families to stay engaged and informed. The best way to stay informed is to register on the IAHE's website for our enewsletter the IAHE Weekly Update. Registering on our website is also the easiest way to sign-up for *The Informer* magazine. It is our goal to present families with the most complete and up-to-date information at all times. Home schools in Indiana are subject to Indiana Legal Code, 20-33-2. These requirements are included in multiple articles throughout this edition of *Home Education in Indiana*.

Why Join Hslda?

The **Home School Legal Defense Association** (HSLDA) was founded by two homeschooling dads (Mike Farris and Mike Smith), both attorneys, in 1983, to defend the Constitutional right of parents to teach their children at home. In states where home schooling was actually illegal, their goal was to pass laws to make homeschooling legal. Thanks to HSLDA's hard work, it is now legal to home educate in all 50 states and member families facing legal troubles related to home education can rest easy knowing help is just around the corner should it ever be needed. HSLDA's support comes from member families who pay less than $100 per year (with the IAHE group discount number) for unlimited legal help, including representation in court on matters related to home education if necessary. All of HSLDA's attorneys are homeschooling dads themselves.

HSLDA advocates on the legal front by fully representing member families at every stage of the proceedings. Each year, thousands of member families receive legal consultation by letter and phone, hundreds more are represented through negotiations with local officials, and dozens are represented in court proceedings. HSLDA also takes the offensive, filing actions to protect members against government intrusion and to establish legal precedent. On occasion, HSLDA will handle precedent-setting cases for non-members as well.

HSLDA advocates on Capitol Hill by tracking federal legislation that affects homeschooling and parental rights. HSLDA works to defeat or amend harmful bills, but also works proactively, introducing legislation to protect and preserve family freedoms.

Home School Legal Defense Association... tens of thousands of American families working through more than 50 dedicated staff members to preserve each other's right to homeschool... together, "Advocates for Family & Freedom." For more information: hslda.org

Providing an Equivalent Education

Debi Ketron

One of the benefits of home education is the ability to tailor your child's education to his or her specific needs. When one follows traditional textbooks and learning styles, it is not difficult to document that education is taking place. One of the methods that home educators may choose to implement is delight-directed learning. Some may use the term "unschooling" due to the fact that it does not appear to be like a traditional education. Many homeschoolers may use delight-directed learning in their homeschool to at least some extent.

A question that must be considered by home educators is: How can one determine that they are providing an "equivalent education" as is required in Indiana Code? (IC 20-33-2-28)

IAHE asked an attorney, Tj Schmidt of Home School Legal Defense Association (HSLDA), about how to define an equivalent education. He said,

> *Indiana law does not explain what 'equivalent instruction' means and the Indiana Department of Education does not have the authority to determine what that is. It is something that would be determined on a case-by-case basis if there were questions as to whether a child was being educated.*
>
> *In these situations, the courts will typically use the common meaning of the word. The Merriam-Webster Dictionary states that 'equivalent' is 'equal in force, amount, or value.' Therefore, a parent teaching their child at home could demonstrate they were providing equivalent instruction by demonstrating they had provided instruction to their child for the same amount of time as the public school. Another option would be to demonstrate that the type of instruction materials they were using were just as comprehensive as those provided in the public school. Finally, they could show that the actual instruction was producing results (i.e. that their child was on/above grade level for their age/abilities).*

HSLDA also recommends that families follow the same general subjects that would be taught in public school, and must teach in the English language. Schmidt continues, "As far as keeping records, Indiana state law only requires attendance records (i.e. the first suggestion listed above-same number of days of instruction). HSLDA does recommend that parents keep (detailed) records of the instruction completed for the current school year just to aid in the event of any challenge to their homeschool program."

These detailed records should include:

- Attendance records

- Information on textbooks and workbooks that your student used

- Portfolios of work

- Samples of schoolwork

- Test results

- Records of any correspondence with school officials

- Any documents that demonstrate that your child is receiving an appropriate education in compliance with the law.

Records should be kept for at least two years. High school records and any home education notification with the State of Indiana (if you choose to report enrollment) should be kept permanently.

Recommended resource to aid in documenting delight-directed learning:

Senior High: A Home-Designed Form+u+la, Barbara Edtl Shelton

Secondary School Recordkeeping to Demonstrate an Equivalent Education

As we consider what it means to provide an "equivalent education", we need to consider our student's possible post-secondary education. Even though the student may not desire a college education at eighteen, he may change his mind in a few years. As home educators, it is crucial that we maintain solid records. When we decide to home educate, we agree to responsibly oversee and implement our child's education. It is a serious proposition that is not to be taken lightly. Homeschoolers need to be provide their student with an equivalent education to the public school even though the specifics are not mandated. IAHE believes that flexibility for each student enables us to provide a superior education.

Many families home educate because they don't want their child to settle for an equivalent education to the public schools. They desire a superior education! Only parents know what that may mean for their child. The most important thing parents can do is to teach their child how to learn and teach to mastery, so that the student actually understands the material and doesn't only learn the information for a test. By the time a student graduates from high school, he needs to know how to teach himself. The student needs to be able to learn from a book or teach himself without having to rely on someone else to "spoon-feed" the information to him. This will truly prepare him for college and for life.

As private schools, Indiana homeschool families determine their own criteria for graduation and issue their student's diploma. Many families use the Indiana Department of Education's diploma standards as a guide. Although Indiana's CORE 40 requirements are not mandated for homeschoolers, Indiana college admission departments may require a student to follow the Indiana CORE 40 requirements as a minimum. One of the advantages of following the Core 40 with academic honors is that it will prepare you for the rigors of college. If a student would like to be considered for an honors college, Indiana's "Core 40 with Academic Honors" is the recommended guideline to follow. Many Indiana home educators follow the honor diploma requirements to best prepare their student for college.

A sample of high school records would be the following sample course descriptions accompanied by the high school transcript. Some colleges may ask for this information and some may not.

English III (1 credit)

A very thorough study of American literature from the Colonial-Revolutionary period through Modern, including an examination of the works in relation to the author's lives and beliefs and in light of the period in which they wrote. More than seventy authors are included, and critical attention is given to movements such as romanticism, Darwinism, and religious liberalism. Grammar and punctuation are reviewed and vocabulary is further developed. Formal essay writing skills are practiced.

Textbooks:

Jensen, Frode. Grammar. Grants Pass, OR: WORDSMITHS, 2003.

Jensen, Frode. Punctuation. Grants Pass, OR: WORDSMITHS, 2003.

Levine, Harold; Levine, Norman; & Levine, Robert T. Vocabulary for the College Bound. New York, NY: Amsco School Publications, Inc., 1993.

Orgel, Joseph R. Scholastic Aptitude Vocabulary. Cambridge, MA: Educators Publishing Services, Inc., 1993.

Payne, Lucile Vaughan. The Lively Art of Writing. Chicago, IL: Follett Publishing Company, 1996.

St. John, Raymond A. American Literature for Christian Schools. Greenville, SC: BJU Press, 2003.

Algebra I (1 credit)

The student will study algebra and develop problem-solving skills. The topics studied include functions, algebraic expressions, systems of equations and their solutions, inequalities, polynomials, ordered pairs, Cartesian coordinate system, quadratic equations, probability, square roots/higher ordered roots, geometric solids, uniform motion problems, Pythagorean theorem, slope-intercept method of graphing, and graphs of linear/non-linear equations.

Text:

Clark, Thomas E. Algebra: A Complete Course. 2nd. Ed. Indianapolis, IN: VideoText Interactive, DVD and books, 2000.

Chemistry/Lab* (1 credit)

The class and lab introduces students to chemistry. Topics include measurement and units; energy, heat, and temperature; atoms and molecules; classifying matter and its changes; counting molecules and atoms in chemical equations, stoichiometry, atomic structure, molecular structure, poly atomic ions and molecular geometry; acid/base chemistry, chemistry of solutions, the gas phase, thermodynamics, kinetics, chemical equilibrium, and reduction/oxidation reactions. Labs include air has mass, air takes up space, comparing conversions to measurements, density of liquids, calibrating the thermometer, measuring the heat capacity of a metal, distinguishing between chemical and physical change, condensing steam in an enclosed vessel, measuring the width of a molecular, limiting reactants, electrical charge, how the eye detects color, polar covalent versus purely covalent compounds, solubility of ionic compounds, acids and bases, acid/base titration, effect of temperature on solid and gaseous solutes, investigation of a solute that releases heat, freezing point depression, using the ideal gas law, determining ΔH of a chemical reaction, factors that affect chemical reaction rates, effect of a catalyst, and invisible writing.

Textbook:

Wile, Jay L. Exploring Chemistry with Creation. 2nd Ed. Anderson, IN: Apologia Educational Ministries, Inc., 2003.

*Note that documenting labs as a part of the science class is extremely important for college admission.

Making a Smooth Transition

Transferring a student from the public school system to homeschool is usually a very simple process. Increasingly, we are finding a lot misinformation and confusing advice both on the Internet and from public school personnel. In Indiana, homeschools are considered non-accredited, nonpublic schools. Legal problems in Indiana are infrequent, but membership in HSLDA ensures proper legal counsel if necessary. To see a complete explanation of Indiana law, see the Home School Legal Defense Association website.

"withdraw" Vs. "Transfer"

Since Indiana law classifies home schools as nonpublic (private) schools we recommend that families use the term "transferring" to a home school instead of "withdrawing" a student from school. While it may seem like a small distinction, this more accurately reflects the shift in the student's status.

Transfer Letter

When transferring a student from the public school system, families should submit a transfer letter to their school principal.

The following transfer letter may be used as a sample. This sample is included for informational purposes only. Every family's situation is different, and you may wish to obtain legal advice.

(Your Street Address)

(Your City, Indiana Zip Code)

(Date)

(Old School's Name)

(Street Address)

(City, State Zip Code)

Dear (Principal's Name):

This letter is to inform you that (Child's Name) will be withdrawing from (Old School) effective (date). (Child's Name) will be transferred to (Homeschool Name) which is a private school.

Please send (Child's Name) records to the following address:

(Homeschool Name)

(Street Address)

(City, Indiana Zip Code)

Thank you for your assistance.

Sincerely,

(Parent's Name)

Reporting to the State of Indiana

Families that seek to remove their child from the public school system are often told that they are **required** to register their homeschool with the Indiana Department of Education. **This is not true**. *There is no registration process for homeschools in Indiana.* However, the Department of Education does allow families to report enrollment. The decision to report to the state is up to each family and should be carefully weighed based on your specific situation. We are not attorneys and can not advise you whether you should or shouldn't report. We recommend contacting HSLDA if you have any questions.

Transferring a High School Student

Effective July 1, 2013, a new law was put in place in an attempt to solve the problem of high school dropouts who are being categorized by the public school as homeschoolers. When a family seeks to withdraw their student from a public high school school, the school is required to provide families with counseling and information about Indiana law on home education (non-accredited, private schools). The school will present families with a form that should be filled out to acknowledge that they understand Indiana law on home education.

THIS APPLIES TO HIGH SCHOOL STUDENTS ONLY:

Section 10 of House Enrolled Act 1005, added I.C. 20-33-2-28.6, a new section, to law. I.C. 20-33-2-28.6 provides the following: (a) This section applies to a high school student who is transferring to a nonaccredited nonpublic school. (b) Before a student withdraws from a public school, the principal of the student's school shall provide to the student and to the student's parent information on a form developed by the department and approved by the state board that explains the legal requirements of attending a nonaccredited nonpublic school located in Indiana.

The principal and a parent of the student shall both sign the form to acknowledge that the parent understands the content of the form. (c) If the parent of the student refuses to sign the form provided by the principal under subsection (b), the student is considered a dropout and the principal shall report the student to the bureau of motor vehicles for action under section 28.5(g) of this chapter. The student is considered a dropout for purposes of calculating a high school's graduation rate under IC 20-26-13-10.

Advice for NEW HOMESCHOOLERS

1 Don't compare your family to others.

2 Focus on mastery and learning, not grades.

3 When trying to decide if public school is no longer for you, don't dismiss your gut

4 You know your child the best and therefore you can do this!!!

5 Decompress. Spend some time at the library and get to know each other again.

6 Don't give up too soon... there will be some bumps and challenges along the way.

7 Don't make "public school" in your home and don't make your school look like anyone else's.

8 When things start to get overwhelming, stop, breathe, and pray.

9 This is now your job, so start each day with a schedule and a routine.

10 Take the time to write down the reasons why you made the decision to homeschool... and review them each year.

Indiana Association of Home Educators

Getting Started

Trust in the Lord with all your heart,
and do not rely on your own understanding.
Acknowledge him in all your ways,
and he will make your paths straight.

Proverbs 3:5–6

A Quick Primer on Choosing Curriculum

Sherrie Payne

One aspect of home education that can be overwhelming for new or experienced home educators alike is deciding on curriculum. With the increase in families choosing home education over the past decade, the curriculum providers have more than met the demand for homeschool resources and supplies. Companies that were in business many years ago have increased their choices, and many new companies have formed. This means families have an abundance of resources to choose from. But this abundance can add to the stress of planning. Sherrie Payne, former IAHE board member, wrote the following article for the original edition of Home Education in Indiana.

I once heard a comparison made between newlyweds at the grocery store for the first time and new homeschooling parents at their first curriculum fair. Both are aware that they need to "stock their shelves". Both often have little idea of the cost or value on the products they are after. The young newlyweds usually have no idea about the differences between the various name brands vs. generic brands and whether fresh, frozen or canned is the best choice for their family's situation. New homeschoolers also have similar choices in curriculum, often confused by the large "name-brand" curriculum offerings and the lesser-known, but often value-packed choices; they may not understand the difference between unit studies, self-paced workbooks and traditional textbooks. The newlyweds at the grocery store will also be confronted with decisions regarding condiments, spices and other seasonings that have the potential to make an otherwise bland meal a gourmet feast. The homeschooler is confronted with similar choices. Once the basic curriculum is decided on and purchased, there are many options to consider that, like condiments and spices, can turn a possible bland lesson into an exciting learning experience.

One other area that both the newlyweds and new homeschoolers need to consider is their personal philosophy regarding the task at hand. For example, when shopping for groceries, we choose those items which match what we think is important regarding food. If we are health conscious, we will shop for fresh or frozen fruits and vegetables, bread products will be wholegrain ingredients, and we will avoid processed foods and preservatives. If convenience is important, then we will choose many ready-made courses, dry cereals, and other items which will take little preparation. And some of us may even be the "fast-food" type, who prefer to eat out and only stock our kitchen pantries with snacks and the bare necessities.

In the same way, we each have a philosophy regarding learning. And the publishers of curriculum also have an educational philosophy. The trick is to match your philosophy with the philosophy of your curriculum. When this happens, both parent and child are much happier with school efforts.

So how can you determine what your educational philosophy is? For starters, give some thought to the following schooling situations:

1. *If you lean towards this philosophy, you believe that there is a basic and essential body of knowledge that a student needs to learn during his school years. The teacher is one who has already mastered this knowledge and his/her job is to transfer this knowledge to the student. The teacher and student have defined roles, i.e., the teacher picks the learning material and then carefully organizes and plans the lessons for the student. The focus is on the subject at hand; textbooks are heavily used and projects are usually viewed as something "extra".*

2. *This view of learning takes a broader view than #1. Learning is not something that is "prepackaged" for those aged 5 to 18 to delve into, but rather something that one pursues throughout his entire life. The liberal arts are valued, so there is an emphasis on classical literature, history and the fine arts. Textbooks and tests will typically not be used in this school, but a freedom of reading choices will fill the student's time. The teacher is viewed as an authority, but not so much as might happen in philosophy #1.*

3. *The focus for this philosophy is on learning about your world through problem solving. Learning is done by doing; the student actively participates in the lesson. Learning material is chosen as needed and involves both teacher and student. Textbooks are not used, no tests given. The distinction between individual subjects is rather fuzzy; instead, the subjects tend to flow together giving an integrated approach to learning.*

4. *This last school of thought is child-centered in every way. There is an emphasis on giving the student choice in what he/she wants to learn. The teacher assumes no authority in the educational role. If the student wants a particular book, only then will books be involved. There is very little, if any, advanced planning on the teacher's part. The teacher only assists as the student needs guidance.*

These four views are a rough generalization of some of the more common educational philosophies. Education textbooks have sophisticated titles for them, but to keep things *simple* let's just label them this way. Philosophy #1 is commonly called the traditional approach to education. This is what most of us were educated under. We had teachers, textbooks for each subject and detailed lesson plans. Learning took place in a formal environment: the classroom. The occasional field trips grew more rare as we grew older.

Since this is the way most of us were raised, it is often times the way we feel most comfortable handling our homeschool situation. The teacher/parent who prefers a more structured environment and is more secure with consistent, regular assignments (including tests for evaluating progress) will most likely have few problems choosing curriculum from this category. The most prominent publishers who also have this same educational philosophy are A Beka Book Publishers, Bob Jones University Press, Rod and Staff Publishers and Saxon. Material can be purchased directly from them. Used book companies who carry homeschool curriculum will also carry this material.

Philosophy #2, the approach that is much broader than the traditional approach, really should be subdivided into at least three or four major thoughts. However, that would best be covered at another time, so only two examples will be given at this time: the Classical approach and the Charlotte Mason approach. Though they differ in the process, both are similar in that the emphasis is on reading excellent literature – the classics of "living books". If this sounds like your style, then check out these major suppliers: Sonlight Curriculum and Simply charlotte Mason.

Philosophy #3 is associated with the unit study approach. In this reasoning, the parent/teacher views knowledge as being interrelated, so learning is centered around a topic or theme, rather than divided into separate subjects. Being actively involved in the learning process is also important, so there is much hands-on activity with this approach. Major unit studies suppliers are KONOS Curriculum and Weaver.

Philosophy #4 is often called the unschooling approach. In this situation, the parent/teacher sees her role as a model for her child as one of an attitude of interest and curiosity in the world around them. The goal is to create in the student an understanding that learning is an integral part of life. The teacher's job is to surround the child with a rich assortment of books and experiences and then be available to answer questions or discuss what the child is interested in. Some families chose to approach education in this manner during the early elementary years, and then move toward a more structured routine as they mature. If more information is wanted in this area, John Holt's books: Teach Your Own and Growing Without Schooling can be found in most libraries.

For a broader list of curriculum providers, and the philosophy they adhere to, read the books Cathy Duffy's *101 Top Picks for Homeschool Curriculum* and *102 Top picks for Homeschool Curriculum*.

Record Keeping - Homeschool Style

Sherrie Payne

You may have already begun your school year. Your books have been collected and the lesson planning has begun. Your school work area has been cleared out, cleaned out and organized; your record keeping system is totally in order.

If the above paragraph is true for you, then read no further. Congratulations! However, if you have started another year with stacks of material on top of your file cabinet rather than in it, and record keeping is something you have for your tax accountant, maybe you should read on.

"Organization and Record Keeping" are two topics that are often linked together. It is true that "organization" is a gift, but it is also true that "orderliness" is a godly character trait – a goal we all should strive toward. I will try to answer some common questions about record keeping, one aspect of an orderly homeschool.

Why Should I Keep Records?

Record keeping is important for two basic reasons. First, keeping accurate records is one proof of not only your child's efforts, but yours. Secondly, there are certain records which are required by Indiana state law. In Indiana, all children between the ages of 7 and 17 are obligated to have an attendance record kept of the 180 days of required school time. Even though very few parents are asked to produce these records, this is a responsibility that we should take seriously. Listed below are areas where some type of record should be maintained. I have also included some suggestions about ways to handle the task.

What Records Should Be Kept?

Attendance – The required attendance record does not have to be elaborate. Some like to use a school calendar with the days checked off or circled. While some prefer to keep track of the days in their lesson plan book, many families keep attendance records separate in case they are ever asked to provide proof of their student's attendance. A simple attendance form is included in the Homeschool Helps section of this book.

School Calendar – I like to keep a yearly calendar of all the extra-curricular activities that round out a child's education. On the calendar I write in such things as field trips, 4-H activities, athletic events, church youth group activities, music/dance lessons, volunteer/service projects, etc.

Lesson Plans - Keep lesson plans in a notebook or regular teacher's plan book.

Elementary (K-8) Subjects – During the elementary years, learning to keep a simple list (by year) of the subjects your students are taking is good practice for what you need to do as they get older. If your curriculum is chosen from several different companies, it is a good idea to include the name of the textbook as well as the publisher after each subject.

High School Courses – If you have high school students (and especially if they are college bound), keep the same list as you would for the elementary grades with the addition of a "course description". A Course description is simply a one-paragraph summary of what is covered in that course, including the textbook name and publisher. An easy way to accomplish this is to use the description found in the catalogue as a guide. If that is not available, use the table of contents of the text. Most colleges that we have dealt with require this. When our first child enrolled in college in 1989, we had not done this. Although I had kept a transcript, I still had to come up with some type of course summary for each course. Needless to say, I spent many hours going back over his four years of high school trying to "catch up" in this area.

Grades – For kindergarten through second grade, a simple checklist of the skills accomplished is sufficient. As you progress through the elementary years, you can use some kind of marks such as 'S' for satisfactory for as long as you and your child are comfortable with this system. If your child has been in another school setting, he may actually prefer to receive letter grades. When you finally do begin giving letter grades, the common standard is the letter 'A' for excellent, 'B' for above average (but not excellent or outstanding), 'C' for average. If you child's work is below these standards, then some evaluation needs to be done. By the time your student is in junior high (grades 6-8), you both should be comfortable with percentage-based letter grades. If you do not know how to figure grades based on percentages, please ask someone. It is a simple mathematical process and I have had many people ask for help with this. Something to consider when giving grades: Many parents do not give grades for the daily work their child does. They feel that this is where the child is doing the learning, so only tests, quizzes, reports, etc... are graded and recorded. I tend to agree with this philosophy. If you have high school students, then percentage-based grades should definitely be kept. These become a part of your student's transcript.

Standardized Test Scores – If your students take achievement tests, be sure to keep their scores in your child's permanent file.

Major School Work File – A file or portfolio should be kept of all your child's major schoolwork. This may include tests, reports, compositions, projects (take pictures and put in the file if necessary). I keep two file folders for each of my children. One file is a *yearly* file labeled with the child's name, grade, and school year. The other folder is a permanent/cumulative file in which I place such items as achievement test reports, newspaper clippings of special awards or activities from club involvement, programs for recitals, recognition forms when they page at the State House. The permanent file is always kept in my file drawer. The yearly file is filed away with that year's lesson plans and school calendar in a box, which I then place in storage. HSLDA recommends that records of this sort be kept for a minimum of three years.

Now, instead of stacking all those papers on top of your file cabinet, I hope these hints help you begin a record-keeping system and help you start your school year off on the right foot.

Sherri Payne and her husband, Rick, served on the Board of Directors of the IAHE. They live near Crawfordsville where they have taught their six children and are now helping homeschool their grandchildren.

Creating an Educational Home

Stacy Hanaway

As homeschoolers, our homes become one large classroom and our lives an educational experience. It is important that we make them as learning friendly as possible. By doing this we create an educational home and lifestyle that will last a lifetime.

One of the goals of many homeschool families is to help foster our children's love of learning that they become lifelong learners. One way of doing this is to make their educational experience a natural way of life. This starts in our home where a child feels safe to explore their world and make the natural connections that will encourage and stimulate their learning.

We start this process often even before birth by reading aloud and surrounding ourselves with music while the child is still in the womb. The next child receives these benefits naturally because parents are doing these activities with older children. As they grow, we encourage learning by books we read, toys we purchase, and music. We are often working with them to learn their ABC's, colors, counting and the foundations of learning. Activities like these should continue and grow with your children and their educational levels. Fill your home with music, posters, games, toys, books, puzzles, and activities that build on these foundations.

In our home, we enjoy games. There are so many different concepts students can learn from simple card and board games. For preschool aged children colors, numbers, letters and patterns. As they move into school age I used these same type card games to teach letter sounds, organization skills, and basic mathematics such as skip counting, missing numbers, simple addition and subtraction. Introduce games where more critical thinking is involved as well as speed, organization, planning, and strategizing. One example is a Go Fish type cards with numbers, letters, shapes, and colors. Start young and basic and then change things up by making the objects a little more difficult. Here is a real life example; I had purchased cards that had capital and lowercase letters. To start I would take 5 cards and match the upper and lower case saying the letter name till I knew they had a grasp on what letters went together. Then we'd play go fish to check their understanding. When they were getting ready to learn to read I then introduced the letters' sounds and play the game using only sounds. You can then use the cards to spell beginning words as well as blends and digraphs. One deck of letter cards can be used to introduce a complete reading and phonics program. With a little imagination this can be applied to many different types of card and board games.

Puzzles are also a wonderful way to encourage many educational concepts. Little hands love puzzles of all shapes and sizes. It is a great way to children to start students learning spatial concepts, critical thinking and organizational skills. Art, geography, and history can lend themselves to instruction through puzzles as well. One example in our home is a three level puzzle of the continental United States. The first level teaches history through land purchases, the next level consist of the states, and finally mountains and other land marks, a whole year's worth of US History from just one puzzle.

Having materials accessible is an important factor in creating an educational home. Allow space for posters with all types of concepts and information from the alphabet and number, to maps, science, math, language arts, timelines, presidents and so much more. Books of all levels, types, sizes, shapes, and subject matter, you can never have too many books. Natural curiosity and continued exposure to these materials encourage students to make them a part of their lives and gives them a confidence in knowing that information is always accessible.

Access to the virtual world, movies, computers, other medias, can be beneficial to your home school. Limit these activities because they can be overdone, however, in the proper context with moderation they can be of beneficial value. Academic competitions such as math, spelling, history or geography bee, science fairs, and 4-H can be used to encourage a student's love of learning. Competitions encourage students to dig deeper and take ownership of what they are learning.

Whether it is trips to the store, field trips, day trips, or vacations take your students to places that they have learned about. There are so many great areas to visit within a day's travel here in the Midwest, such as caverns, plantations, zoos, museums, farms, fair, battle fields, and parks. We also make a point of our vacations having a history and geography lesson built in them. There are a great set of books written by George and Michele Zavatsky, all titled Kids Love... packed with fun and inexpensive trip ideas for families. I would encourage you to look them up; their website even has a whole home school section.

By creating an educational home, we then encourage our children's natural curiosity and allow them to make natural connections in learning. This will give your students ownership in their education and become lifelong learners.

Jason & Stacy Hanaway are the Lead Regional Representatives for IAHE. They live with their two sons, on a small farm in LaGrange County. They have been homeschooling for the past seven years. Jason is in management with INDOT. Stacy has taught in parochial, public school, and now homeschool! They feel blessed to be called to homeschool.

10 Do's and Don'ts for New Homeschoolers

Annette Breedlove

Are you thinking of homeschooling this year, but don't know where to start? It can be overwhelming to say the least. Homeschooling isn't something that comes naturally to most of us. In fact, it's a lot of work. But with a few helpful tips, you might feel more at ease in starting your homeschool journey.

10 Things You Need to Know Before Starting Homeschooling

1. Do ask questions.

Asking questions is always a good place to start. And you're sure to have many as you embark on this new journey called homeschooling. There is so much information out there it's easy to confuse a veteran, let alone a newbie. But where do you start? I suggest starting with your friends who homeschool and those who have similar family values and philosophies. They are more likely to line up with what you want to do in your own homeschool and it will give you a good place to start. Some questions you might ask are:

- Do you follow a homeschool methodology?

- What is your favorite curriculum and why?

- What subjects do you teach?

- How do you structure your homeschool day?

- Do your kids participate in any extracurricular activities?

2. Don't over research.

A dangerous trap that many new homeschoolers, including myself, fall into is over researching. Asking questions is one thing, but asking and asking and asking without making any decisions can lead to confusion. While researching more and more might seem like a good thing, the old saying, "too much of a good thing is bad," comes to mind. I did this before our first year and found myself scrambling at the last minute to find curriculum and products to use. Do your homework and then make some decisions. The good thing about homeschooling is you can change things up if you find they're really not a good fit for your child's learning style.

3. Do write out your philosophy and goals.

Sit down and write out the reasons why you want to homeschool. What is your goal? What is your philosophy about homeschooling – both in general and personally? Then discuss them with your spouse and/or a homeschool friend. Tweak them as needed and then post them somewhere you will see them. Not only will this help you in your curriculum choices, it will also help you stay focused on why you are on this journey. It is also a good way to refocus on those difficult days, which will happen. Every year, re-evaluate your goals and philosophy to make sure they are still in line with what you want for you homeschool. This will keep your homeschool fresh and new as well as productive.

4. Don't wing it.

Although I'm sure there have been some very successful homeschoolers with this philosophy, I don't recommend it. This is where I got into trouble our first year. I thought we could just pick out some age and grade appropriate curriculum and then go for it. Did my son learn? Yes. Did he learn all he could, if I would have had a plan? I don't think so. Since then I have outlined our philosophies and goals as well as our curriculum and we have accomplished much more than I ever thought possible.

5. Do make a plan for the year.

Even though we follow a somewhat child-led philosophy, we still make a plan for what we want to study. Whether you plan weekly, monthly, semi-annually or by the year, make a plan for what you want to cover. What subjects you want to teach. And what you want to accomplish by the end of the year. Keep in mind this may change throughout the year, but at least you have a plan from which to work and move forward.

6. Don't over plan.

In the beginning I would spend hours and even days writing out plans for our homeschool. And with one child, it worked. We stayed on track pretty well and we covered quite a bit of subjects. He learned at a quicker pace on some subjects than I expected, but that was easy to remedy. However, once I added in our two middle children, the plans I had outlined didn't work. We didn't cover the subjects I wanted to cover in a day, let alone each week. We fell further and further behind and all it did was frustrate me and the kids. So I learned to follow their lead and take my cues from them. If they wanted to do more "papers" that day, we did. If they wanted to work on math, we did. While I have a goal in mind for each day, we now spend more time where it's needed rather than on "completing assignments" for the sake of a checklist.

7. Do keep records.

If your state requires you keep records, this is a must. However, some states do not require records be kept or submitted, so some parents just don't worry about it. I would highly recommend you keep records – even if just for yourself. First of all, there is no guarantee that your states laws won't change in the future, which means they can come after you for past records. Second, it helps you and your child see how far they have come. It shows where they have improved and where they still need to improve. Records can also help you see where changes might need to be made in curriculum and/or structure.

8. Don't throw everything away.

Even though you might keep records, that doesn't mean you should throw everything away. In fact, I highly recommend you don't. I don't keep everything, but I do keep certain things for nostalgia reasons and certain things for the sake of record-keeping. For instance, handprints and footprints. I keep all art projects involving their handprints and footprints and I make sure to date them. As for their tests, I keep all spelling, grammar and math tests in these early years. I imagine that will grow as we do more subjects and take more advanced subjects. I also keep their handwriting papers – partly for nostalgia and partly for record-keeping. When they complain that their handwriting is awful or isn't getting better, we look back on past papers to see just how far they have come. This is a great encouragement to them and me both.

9. Do watch for sales.

Once you have outlined your goals and philosophies, it is time to start shopping. First, make sure you ask around and find out where to find curriculum on sale and the best times to buy. Some homeschool groups offer sale dates at their meetings and some offer sales on their Facebook pages. If you're looking for a specific curriculum, sometimes there are Facebook buy/sell groups for them and you can pick up some pretty good deals. Homeschool sites have deals throughout the year, but most of them you can find sales in April/May and during the Christmas holiday. Many companies offer discounts and free shipping on purchases made at the Annual IAHE Convention. I usually try to plan our next year's curriculum in time to hit the sales in the Spring and then if we need to purchase more or change our course, I can buy on sale again during the holiday sales. It has worked out nicely for us and saved us quite a bit of money too.

10. Don't overpay.

Watching for sales is key to keeping your homeschool costs to a minimum. However, sometimes it is not possible to get curriculum on sale or at a discount. And that's where price comparison comes into play. Do your research and find out what prices each competitor offers. My usual sites are Amazon, Timberdoodle and of course, the individual curriculum sites. As I mentioned before, I can be a bit of an over planner, so I have a spreadsheet set up where I track prices. That way if I see a product come up for sale during the year, I have a point of reference. It also helps me when I'm tracking the sales and Facebook groups. I know what the original prices are and I know what I'm willing to pay on sale.

Being a homeschool family doesn't mean you need to take out a second mortgage on the house. It also doesn't need to be stressful.

With these 10 Tips, I'm sure your homeschool year will be a success!

Annette has been married to her husband and best friend for 12+ years. Together they are raising their four children, with a new one arriving late July 2016, to follow the Lord's will, no matter what. Annette longs for the day when she will meet each of her angel babies who have entered heaven before her. She enjoys creating FREE PRINTABLES for homeschool families for her own children and her readers. She blogs at In All You Do (www.inallyoudo.net) where she talks about homeschooling, gluten- and grain-free recipes (when she cooks), homemaking, Biblical marriage, the occasional DIY projects and maintaining her sanity.

Teacher's Toolbox

Building Blocks for Toddlers

Sherrie Payne

T his past summer I did what I usually do. Before the start of school, I cleaned and reorganized my schoolroom. And I did something else. I packed up all my materials that I had used when my children were toddlers, and preschoolers and put them in boxes for storage. With our youngest almost sixteen years old, I thought it was probably a little overdue!

But as I was packing each item away-games, books, curriculum, even toys-the memories em flooding back from the time we first began homeschooling. Fifteen years ago, our 'classroom' contained a 9-month old baby, a 3-year old toddler, a 4 1/2-year old preschooler, a kindergartner, and a 2nd grader (a 6th grader was still in public school at the time). Since I knew of no other homeschool family, I had no idea what I was getting into.

It didn't take long, however, to get a feel for what my days would be like. I knew I had to decide on several things right away. When would we begin our school day? How long was 'enough'? What would I do with the younger ones? And most of all, with three little ones, how was I going to keep my sanity? Many times, I have been asked, "How did you manage!" For those of you who are now in the position that our family was back then, I would like to pass on some things that time has shown to be effective.

Structure

I found that having a structure to our school day helped the children know what to expect. From the very beginning, the word' school' meant being in a specific area to perform specific tasks at a specific point in time. Now, before you 'un-schoolers' tune me out, let me explain.

From my perspective, as a teacher/mom, 'school' is never over; I am always aware of the teachable moment. But with the children, I found that they were much more settled when they were in a routine that included a time and place to do their 'school' duties, i.e., math work, spelling tests, etc.

So our school day would begin sometime after breakfast and the necessary morning chores were finished. For our family, that would be sometime between 9 and 10 in the morning. But when Mom said, "Time for school!", everyone (including the dog!) knew where we were headed and what we'd be doing for the next two or three hours. The baby was placed on a blanket on the floor nearby; the toddler and preschooler knew what toys and activities were available for them during school time. They even had their own desks and would use them when they wanted to do 'school work'.

Expectations

My parenting style has sometimes been compared to that of a drill sergeant (which I don't consider especially flattering), but I have seen some positive results from one aspect. Children tend to live up to expectations we set before them. Expectations should not only be realistic, but also identifiable and enforceable. For literally years, our Bible study lesson was focused on some aspect of character building. The children, both young and old, learned about obedience, attentiveness, patience, initiative, diligence. They memorized a definition for each character trait as well as an appropriate Bible verse. We read Bible stories about people who were examples of the trait and did various activities. Once the trait was learned (we'd spend one week on each trait each year), than I expected that trait to have a developing presence in each child

Looking back, I think God had us learn these traits because Mom needed them as much as the children. I needed to know that obedience means, "doing what you're told immediately, thoroughly, and with a happy spirit" so that I could live it and expect it from my children. I also needed to know that diligence means "doing a task in a way that pleases the Lord," so that I could focus on doing what God expects of me as well as expect that our children complete their chores and school work.

When it was time for school, the younger ones knew that I would be working mostly with their school- age siblings; however, they wanted and needed my attention, too. I was very firm with them about my expectations. They were not to be loud, running around the house or whining (I never allowed whining).

On the other hand, I acknowledged their presence in the room by commenting on such things as how high their block tower was, or what a nice dress their baby doll had on, or suggesting an activity when I saw one getting restless. Yes, it took patience, attentiveness, and energy on my part, but I am absolutely convinced now that this is the reason God gives babies to young people.

Vision

Most of you are familiar with Proverbs 22:6: "Train up a child in the way he should go: and when he is old, he will not depart from it." I once heard a teaching on this verse, which says that this means to look for the bents (God-given gifts, talents) that a child has and work with those bents to develop that bent by telling him how much it pleases both his earthly parents and his heavenly Father. Look for ways in which your child can utilize that gift.

Again, focused character building is your young ones (approximately 3 years old and up) is of the utmost importance. Having a general vision for what is godly, then transferring that vision to your children through your expectations will in time produce good fruit in both behavior and spiritual giftings.

So the bottom line from this 'older woman' is: Make a sincere effort to provide structure-a place and time. Then let God guide your expectations and allow Him to give you a vision for His plans and purpose for each of your children.

Oh, by the way, I didn't put those boxes in the attic. Our oldest daughter is finishing college with a degree in early childhood education. And besides her, I have a three-year old grandson and five-year old granddaughter! Let's see ... maybe I should just move them to ... my son's house or my daughter's dorm room?

{Sample} Elementary Scope and Sequence

The "scope and sequence" of curricula are generally accepted guidelines followed in planning a child's area of study. Appropriate maturational and intellectual levels are considered in the designing of these guidelines and the following lists contain examples of concepts that may be covered at different grade levels. A child should always be allowed to progress at their own rate. Some children may be ahead of the following schedule for their age group while others may be behind. The next few pages should be used only as a *guide* to the equivalency of a grade level in the public schools. Parents should always be aware that a child should not be pushed beyond his ability, but at the same time, many children need to be challenged to use the abilities the Lord has given them. It takes discernment on the part of the parent to meet each individual need appropriately – to challenge each at just the right time and in just the right way to make learning a wonderful adventure.

Reading

Kindergarten – 1st Grade

The term "readiness" refers to those activities (mostly structured) of the preschool or early elementary age child that actually prepare him to learn to read and understand beginning math concepts. These activities start when you hold your child on your lap, read to him and talk about the pictures. He learns to hold a book, turn pages, and sees left to right sequencing. HE soon learns to relate written and spoken language. Through discussion of the story he builds his vocabulary and begins to develop reading comprehension skills. Sorting, matching, and discriminating between objects in games are other readiness activities that come along in normal playtime. Learning the sounds and names of letters (magnetic letters are great) along with matching beginning and ending sounds through audio or visual discrimination are also important activities for the younger child. Preschool children can easily be encouraged to make up simple stories or retell a familiar story. Wholesome family activities (a trip to a museum, park, or zoo, of baking cookies) expose the child to new learning experiences, build vocabularies, and make learning a fun family event.

Initial Steps to Reading:

Learn the sounds of letters (vowels first); the names of the letters of the alphabet; recognize that sounds make up words; recognize upper and lowercase letters; learn to blend the letters; recognize simple words; and recognize blends, digraphs and diphthongs (not the terms). If the child is progressing well he should be able to: recognize basic sight words; recognize root words/base words; recognize some suffixes; be able to read aloud and indicate the end of a sentence by voice inflections; and be able to recognize new words in context.

2nd and 3rd Grades

By this level the child should be increasing his sight vocabulary, comprehension skills, and solidifying his understanding of phonics. Children should be able to: independently read for enjoyment; follow written instructions; understand, read and write contractions and compound words; understand and count syllables in at least two syllable words; understand and relate story sequence; recognize homonyms, synonyms and antonyms; use basic phonics skills consistently; recognize common suffixes and prefixes; and consistently expand their vocabulary.

4th – 6th Grades

Although still limited by maturity level and lack of knowledge, a child at this grade level should be able to read most written material. Some children might need remedial attention while most will be reading for information and pleasure. Advanced reading skills should include: reading with increasing skill and expression; following more difficult written instructions; listening to adult reading which improves both reading and listening skills; using reading skills to locate information and for practical reading such as newspapers, advertisements, etc.; understanding prefixes and suffixes on a more difficult level by studying Latin and Greek derivatives; learning dictionary skills; identifying an author's point of view; comparing authors and their works; becoming familiar with renowned authors and their works; reading and studying a variety of forms of prose and poetry; analyzing reading material for theme, appeal, technique, and effectiveness; and reading for literary value.

7th and 8th Grades

General literature: There are many excellent literature texts available. Students should be reading from classic and contemporary novels.

Grammar and Composition

Kindergarten – 1st Grade

Students should learn to: speak in complete sentences; follow oral directions; tell stories; say name, address and telephone number; recognize rhymes; listen to others reading; relate simple stories, verses and rhymes orally; write simple sentences ending with periods; and capitalize first letters of sentences and proper names.

2nd – 3rd Grades

Students should learn to: follow oral and written directions; use the suffixes: -s, -ed, -ing and some prefixes; use apostrophes; alphabetize; recognize syllables; use a dictionary; write simple stories, notes, and reports; punctuate sentences using periods, question marks, commas, and exclamation points; capitalize proper nouns and words at the beginning of sentences; understand what a complete sentence is; and identify the following parts of speech: nouns, verbs, adjectives and simple conjunctions.

4th Grade

Students should learn to: participate in discussion; write simple stories, poems, letters, reports, etc; apply punctuation rules for: periods, commas, exclamation points, question marks, periods after abbreviations, initials and commas in a series, dates, greetings and closings of letters; identify possessive words; properly use apostrophes; group related sentences to form a paragraph; write a letter and address an envelope; use capitalization rules; identify: nouns, verbs (state of being and action), pronouns, adjectives, conjunctions; and recognize and diagram indirect objects and prepositional phrases.

5th Grade

Students should learn to : give oral reports; use all punctuation correctly including quotation marks; underline titles; write reports (2-5 pages), letters, prose, poetry, creative stories; proofread and edit their own work; identify nouns, verbs, adjectives, adverbs, pronouns; identify subjects, predicates and direct objects; recognize subject-predicate agreement; use adjectives and adverbs in writing; apply correct usage of verbs; identify prepositions, conjunctions and interjections; recognize agreement between pronouns and antecedents; learn irregular plurals; diagram subjects and verbs, direct objects, adjectives and adverbs, prepositions and conjunctions; and recognize and diagram indirect objects and prepositional phrases.

6th – 8th Grades

Student should learn to: give oral reports and participate in group discussions; use plural possessives and contractions; recognize and write compound sentences; write outlines and topic sentences; compose poetry, short research papers, book reports, dialogue; write with unity and coherence; proofread and edit their own work; develop total understanding of use of dictionary; understand appositives and direct address ("you"); master helping and linking verbs; write compositions; identify simple verbs (can be taught as early as 4th grade); use predicate adjective and predicate nominative; diagram all the parts of speech; define and learn examples of similes and metaphors; use a thesaurus; and take notes from printed and oral material.

Mathematics

Kindergarten

Begin by working with the student on: relating quantities (same/different, larger/smaller, shorter/taller, long/ longer/ longest); classifying (by color, shape, size, common characteristics); relating characteristics (matching items one for one, recognizing like amounts, duplicating a given pattern); recognizing basic shapes (square, circle, rectangle, triangle); recognizing and ordering numerals 0-10; counting and printing numerals 0-10, understanding concepts of smaller/larger and more/less involving values from 0 to 10 with aid of pictures; and naming coins (penny, nickel, dime, etc.)

1st Grade

Students should learn to: count, recognize and write numerals 0-100; memorize addition and subtraction of numbers from 0-10; understand place values (ones, tens and hundreds); recognize "greater than" and "less than" concepts, apply simple problem solving; identify fractional shapes and parts of a whole for ½, ¼, and 1/3; measure: 1 cup, ½ cup, foot, inch, yard; and add and subtract two digit numbers without carrying and borrowing.

2nd Grade

Student should: review addition and subtraction facts to 10 + 10; learn carrying and borrowing in math (regrouping); accomplish counting, identifying and writing numerals up to 100; learn to use "greater than" and "less than" symbols; begin learning the concept of multiplication; learn to count by twos, and fives to 100; review place value of hundreds, tens and ones; identify parts and the numerals for ½, 1/3 , ¼ in fractional shapes and fractional parts of a whole; understand money concepts up to $1.00; tell time (hour, half hour and quarter hour); apply measurement (linear, liquid, and weight); interpret simple bar graphs; and solve one-step word problems with either addition or subtraction.

3rd Grade

Student should learn to: multiply up to 9 x 9 (mastery may not come until grade 4); divide (introduced pictorially or with hands on objects); identify place value to thousands and ten thousands; read and write up to five digit numbers; recognize even and odd numbers; add and subtract three digit numbers where regrouping is required; divide with one digit divisor; recall multiplication and division facts up to 9 x 9; multiply one digit times two digits with carrying; identify fractions: ½, 1/3, and ¼ of different shapes and amounts; understand a.m. and p.m. and tell time to the nearest five minutes; identify days and months; count, add and subtract money; use $ and decimal point; measure using linear, liquid, and weight measurements; use the metric system; do one-step problem solving using addition, subtraction, multiplication or division; do simple estimates; make up simple word problems.

4th Grade

Student should learn to: do any addition and subtraction with whole numbers; read and identify any numeral up to seven digits and beyond; do two-digit times three-digit multiplication; round off numbers; learn estimation; divide with two-digit divisors; show remainders in division; add and subtract fractions with like denominators; understand fractions as ratios; reduce fractions; master time (be able to read and write to the nearest minute); count money and make change; master more difficult measurement concepts regarding length and mass; do all liquid measurement; identify all shapes and construct graphs; add and subtract mixed numbers (2 2/3 + 5 1/6); solve more complicated word problems; use data to construct word problems; determine missing data for problem solving; find averages.

5th Grade

Student should learn to: do any addition, subtraction, multiplication, and division problems with whole numbers; add, subtract and multiply any decimals; divide whole numbers by decimals; use ratios; master more difficult measurements; determine prime factors; read and write up to nine digit numbers; use decimals other than in relationship to money; read and write decimals to the thousandths; determine the area of squares and rectangles; introduce the concept of volume with cubes; round off whole numbers and decimals; estimate; identify the following terms: congruence, symmetry, diameter, radius, angle, parallel, perpendicular, and intersecting lines; construct and interpret graphs; compute the area of a triangle; use math to solve real life problems; and use a protractor.

6th Grade

Student should learn to: read and write all decimals; change percents to decimals; understand and apply percentage; introduce integers; read and write all 12 digit numerals; do any computation using fractions and decimals; convert fractions to decimals and decimals to fractions; determine circumference and area of circles; use a protractor to measure and draw angles; interpret graphs; line circle and bar; convert units of measure in the system; quarts to pints, yards to feet, etc.; formulate and apply problem solving strategy; deal with exponential notation; define, explain and use probability; analyze and evaluate statistics.

7th and 8th Grade

Student should study general math or pre-algebra with an emphasis on problem solving using all math concepts.

Social Studies: History, Geography, Government

Kindergarten – 2nd Grade

Focus for the student at this level should be on the neighborhood and town, or rural area and town most frequented. Children should become familiar with surrounding streets and roads and how to get to and from familiar places. Children should be aware of the types of stores in the area and the public services, such as police stations, fire departments, hospitals, libraries, etc. Second grade is a good time to begin map skills (a homemade map of a familiar area is helpful). Children should learn directions (north, south, east, west) around their home and understand those directions on a map. Introduce the timeline concepts using the child's actual birth as the beginning and add events that have happened since the child's birth.

3rd Grade

Students should; study Native Americans including types of shelter, dress, etc.; learn more map skills including roads, towns, lakes, rivers, etc.; study national holidays; begin study of prominent historical figures like Washington, Lincoln, Kennedy, Martin Luther King, Jr., Wright Brothers, etc.; start a timeline and include these people; study different kinds of occupations and interview people working in these fields.

4th Grade

This is the year to study Indiana history. Include materials from first settlement to the present. Students can practice map skills by using a map of Indiana, locating major towns, highways, waterways and surrounding states. They should study famous Indiana people from the past and present. Field trips to the State House and other important historical spots can add much to the course. Include a study of Indiana government.

5th Grade

United States history should be taught this year. It can be taught from a textbook or through unit studies. Helpful ideas include making extensive maps and constructing a timeline. Many read literary works that relate to different periods of time in our country's history. This is a time to practice writing good reports.

6th Grade

Students usually study world history this year. Extensive use of maps can be very helpful. Continue the timeline from previous years. Students should write reports and simple research papers.

7th Grade

During seventh grade world geography is taught, but from the cultural, physical and political aspect.

8th Grade

United States history is taught again this year.

Science

A general science program is taught throughout elementary and middle school years. Science textbooks for each grade level are published by most curriculum companies. The use of a text can insure consistent instruction in this subject. Most texts suggest enrichment reading ideas for experiments and activities. These help the parent motivate the student and allow more first-hand experience for the child than textbook reading. Parents need to take advantage of the child's writing education by requiring reports appropriate to the grade level. Learning the scientific process is also important. Many parents make use of unit studies for science in the elementary grades. This can be an effective way to study science. By involving all of your children, it provides a family activity at the same time.

Note: Cathy Duffy's Christian Home Educators' Curriculum Manual – Elementary Grades is highly recommended for further in-depth study and ideas for teaching grades K-6.

What About Support?

The IAHE recommends that homeschooling families become a part of a local support group. In Indiana there are nearly 250 support groups. They exist to provide encouragement, information, socialization, and friendship for homeschooling families. However, just as homeschools differ, support groups differ. Some are designed for educational purposes. Some focus on field trips or special interests, such as history or drama. Some are educational 'co-op groups where the parents share the teaching responsibilities.

As a means of connecting new homeschoolers to the support needed, the IAHE has selected 16 experienced homeschooling couples as Regional Representatives. Each Representative is a 'veteran' homeschooler who can answer the questions from families just starting out. Regional Representatives also communicate with the local support groups in their region and keep them up to date on changes in in the law and activities throughout the state. You can contact your Regional Representative for information about spelling bees, sports clubs, book fairs, curriculum advice, workshops, standardized testing and convention information. Regional Representatives can also help you find a support group in your area, or if none is available, they'll help you start one.

The Importance of Support Groups

Rebecca Barnes

God never intended for us to do life alone. He wired us to need each other, to need fellowship with like-minded people. That's why we attend the church we do, why we have the friends we have, even why God put us in the family we're in. Our homeschool "families" are no different.

When I first began homeschooling my first child, I was pretty clueless. She struggled with learning—a LOT. I didn't know how to handle that. Plus she was born with Spina Bifida, which was/is a huge medical ordeal. Those first few years of homeschooling were challenging. I often thought that I wasn't qualified to deal with this "special needs" child, and that I should just put her in public school. But I had some pretty fantastic people who supported me and reminded me that this was God's calling on my life. They spurred me on to run the race with perseverance. They were my local support group and my family. We have been fortunate to have the full and unwavering support of both sets of parents, but the support of my local homeschooling friends was even more of a blessing because they have "been there, done that" or were willing to "be there, do that" along with me. There is nothing like having the encouragement of someone who is doing what you're doing and are doing it for similar reasons.

So why are support groups important?

1) **Support groups help us run and finish the race of homeschooling.** Ecc 4:9-12 *"Two are better than one, because they have a good return for their work: if one falls down, his friend can help him up. But pity the man who falls and has no one to help him up! Also, if two lie down together, they will keep warm. But how can one keep warm alone? Though one may be overpowered, two can defend themselves. A cord of three strands is not quickly broken."*

Heb 10:24 *"And let us consider how we may spur one another on toward love and good deeds."*

Heb 12:1 *"Therefore, since we are surrounded by such a great cloud of witnesses, let us throw off everything that hinders, and the sin that so easily entangles, and let us run with perseverance the race marked out for us."*

Support groups are our cheerleaders. They are our coaches. They are our mentors. Support groups help fill the need of fellowship and friendship. In a support group, your children will develop good solid friendships without peer pressure.

2) **Support groups are a natural fit for being a Titus 2 woman.** Titus 2:3-5 *"Older women likewise are to be reverent in behavior, not slanderers or slaves to much wine. They are to teach what is good, and so train the young women to love their husbands and children, to be self-controlled, pure, working at home, kind, and submissive to their own husbands, so that the word of God may not be reviled."* We often see examples of how to teach, how to discipline, and how to interact with our children by simply observing the "seasoned" moms. Often times, I find myself talking with a group of moms and we're all struggling in one area or another. We all share our ideas, share what has worked for us, what hasn't. What curriculum we use, what we've tried and liked, what we've tried and tossed. We also share curricula. Through my group, I've been able to encourage other moms who have a child that struggles with learning. Giving them tips of how to help their child or where to go for help.

3) **Support groups are useful for shared field trips and regular activities.** Yes, you can take your kids to the zoo or the children's museum on your own. My family has done so many times. But sometimes it is more fun to go with a group and it usually has some financial benefit as well. At several places we have been to, the teacher gets in free, the cost for groups of 10 or more is more than half off, and we've even gotten some extra perks for coming as a school group (like a "buy-one-get-one free" return visit coupon). Group field trips create camaraderie with your children as well as the adults attending. My group also has some monthly activities. Throughout the school year we have a monthly skating and library day. We've also had bowling days or park days, just to facilitate fun and friendships.

4) **How to keep a support group going?** This can be a tough one. My own group has experienced growth spurts and then declines. Our group is more of a committee run support group rather than a few people doing it all. I find that when you have more voices in the planning stages of your activities, then you will generally get a good balance of what will meet the needs of most people. It does take a bit of effort, especially when you have a wide variety in ages and grades amongst your children. Our group has every age from toddler to seniors, with the

largest age group being the senior high school range. It's impossible to meet the needs of every member of your group. That's why a variety of people adding input to the planning process each year is so important.

It takes sacrifice sometimes. Let's say a family has elementary age children and wants to have a field trip to the fire station. You've already been to the fire station... twice. But in order to help this other family, you sacrifice an hour of your day to go to the fire station so that this family (and others) can have enough people there to make the field trip a worthwhile experience for them AND for the firefighters that are giving up an hour of their day to give you a tour. It means sometimes you do teen oriented activities when you have elementary age children, or vice versa. But keep in mind that this is yet another opportunity to practice being a Titus 2 woman, by being involved and engaged in other people even though it may not benefit your family as much.

5) **Encouragement to be inclusive.** Being a Region 13 Rep, I see a lot of support groups that are exclusive, private, or even secret. My heart is always sad when I see this happen. I know the reasons: "Our co-op got too big, so we now don't allow anyone new." "We just really like the people that are in the group." "Our group will grow, but by invitation only to insure that they are a good fit for our group." Yes, we all love to be with people we like and are fun to be with and we don't want to add a new element that could potentially disrupt that cohesiveness. I get that. But remember when YOU first started homeschooling and the plethora of help and information that you gained from veteran homeschoolers? That is what a support group is all about! The veteran homeschooling mom encourages the not-so-veteran homeschooling mom, who encourages another mom that she CAN homeschool her kid, then the veteran is encouraged because she has renewed hope that she is doing the right thing.

If you belong to a support group, I encourage you to go out of your way to include new families. It is so awkward, just like attending a new church... you don't know anyone yet and it's just plain hard to walk up to strangers and introduce yourself or jump into friendships. If you don't have a support group, consider starting one. Chances are, there are several other families around that would love to do that too, but don't know where to start. Getting started is pretty easy. You start with a meeting place, invite some people, and let the planning begin. There is a helpful article in the Fall edition of *The Informer* on starting support groups. If you happen to be in a support group that regularly restricts new people from attending group functions, then I encourage you to introduce some changes or offer to start a secondary part of the group to be an encouragement to new families. Remember what is was like when you first started and how the support of others made a difference to you on your journey. Or perhaps, you need to offer that support that you did NOT get, so you can be that difference to someone else's journey. A support group is not a requirement to homeschool, but it certainly makes the journey a little brighter and a bit easier.

Rebecca Barnes, wife to Steve, momma of four daughters, has been home educating since the birth of her first child in 1993. They live on a small farm in rural Randolph County and serve as Region 13 Reps and as local support group leaders. The family loves the closeness that homeschooling affords, as well as the flexibility it can bring. They have homeschooled and graduated two children and have experienced the joys and struggles that go along with educating a child that learns differently. Rebecca loves being an encourager of other families on their homeschool journey.

Frequently Asked Questions

F.A.Q.S: Homeschooling in Indiana

Tj Schmidt, HSLDA

IAHE fields many questions throughout the year related to homeschooling in Indiana. While some of the following information has already been covered in earlier chapters, we wanted to take the opportunity to cover some of the most frequently asked questions from Indiana families.

In 2013, we asked Indiana's HSLDA attorney, Tj Schmidt, to answer the following questions.

1. **IAHE has fielded questions from some who say that there are those who are not teaching their children. What does it mean to provide an "equivalent" education to that of the local public school?**

    Indiana law doesn't define "equivalent" so we look to the common definition of the word. Miriam-Webster defines "equivalent" as "equal in force, amount, or value" or "like in signification or import." Indiana law requires that the instruction is to be equivalent to that given in the public schools. "Instruction" is defined as "the action, practice, or profession of teaching." Thus, in our opinion, a parent can provide equivalent instruction in accordance with Indiana law by teaching their child subjects that are equal in value to what is provided in the public school. A parent does not need to use the same curriculum or even the same methods that are used in the public school. The State Board does not have the authority to define what equivalent instruction is. See also question 7.

2. **Do you advise keeping records in case there is ever a charge of educational neglect? (Over and above attendance records?)**

    Indiana law requires attendance records solely to verify enrollment and attendance of a child in a nonpublic school. It is recommended that a parent keep records that are sufficient to verify "equivalent instruction" has been provided. There is no right or wrong way. However, a parent could keep samples of instruction or work done by the student in each subject regularly throughout the school year. If you have samples from the beginning, middle, and end of the school year you will demonstrate that the child was provided instruction in the various subjects and that they made educational progress.

3. **What public official has the right to look at attendance records?**

    Indiana law only provides that the state superintendent and the superintendent of the local school corporation can legally request the attendance records of a nonpublic school. While other state agencies may ask for evidence that a student is being educated, only the individuals above can request the attendance records of a nonpublic (home)school.

4. How many days a year does the state require us to teach?

Indiana law requires all children of compulsory attendance age to attend school for the same number of days the public schools are in session. Generally, a public school is required to provide 180 instructional days each school year.

5. Is registration of a homeschool on the Indiana Department of Education website required?

No. However, in some situations it may be preferable to indicate that you have registered with the Indiana Department of Education than submit information verifying that you are providing equivalent instruction to your child(ren). Registration is not the same, but some state agencies view it as being the same. A parent is most likely to face pressure to register when a child is withdrawn from a public school.

6. Does the compulsory attendance law apply to homeschoolers?

Yes. Compulsory attendance laws apply to any child from age 7 until 18 (or they have graduated). However, a child attending a nonpublic, non-accredited (home)school is not bound by the curriculum or content of the educational program required to be provided by public schools.

7. Are homeschoolers required to follow the Core 40 requirements for high school?

Homeschoolers are not required to follow the Core 40 and complete the exact credits required to complete a homeschool program in Indiana. They could simply cover the equivalent subjects covered in high school in Indiana. However, a parent who is interested in having their child graduate and attend an Indiana college would benefit from being able to demonstrate that their student completed the appropriate credits listed in the Core 40.

8. If a homeschooler follows the Core 40 with Honors diploma requirements, can a student's transcript say "Honors Diploma" for college?

Just as a homeschool student can't say they have a "Core 40" diploma, they couldn't say they have a "Core 40 Honors Diploma." Those are public school designations. However, if a student has met the credit requirements for either of these diplomas, they can—and should—indicate that what they have completed is equivalent to a "Core 40" diploma or a "Core 40 with Academic Honors" diploma.

9. I had read somewhere that you can put on the homeschool transcript that a class is "honors" but you cannot use the "AP" label because AP is licensed

by the College Board and only classes and curriculum approved by them can be labeled as such. Do you know if this is true?

You can only use the AP label to a course that has been approved by the College Board.

10. **When withdrawing/transferring a student from the public school system, do homeschool parents have the right to request the student's school records?**

Under Indiana law "a public agency must permit the parent, or parent's representative, to inspect and review any educational record of the parent's children for birth to eighteen (18) years of age that are collected, maintained, or used by the public agency." A parent also has the right to request an amendment of educational records. The public agency must allow the parent to inspect and review the educational record without unnecessary delay and in no case more than 45 calendar days after the request is made. The parent also has a right to make copies of the record and they can be charged no more than the actual cost of the copies. See 511 IAC 7-38-1. Federal law has similar provisions for parents to access their children's educational records.

Thomas J. (Tj) Schmidt was first taught at home in the second grade by his parents in northern Vermont. For nearly all of the remaining years of his elementary and secondary education Tj was taught at home. For much of that time his family was on foreign mission fields. Tj received his J.D. while studying at home from Oak Brook College of Law and began serving as a Legal Assistant at HSLDA. Now, as an HSLDA Staff Attorney, Tj answers general legal questions and assists members across the country experiencing legal difficulties.

What about sports?

Some of the most frequently asked questions from homeschool families revolve around finding sports programs for their students.

Indiana is blessed with an abundance of homeschool sports teams organized by volunteer parents across the state. Many communities also have recreational leagues for elementary and middle school students that are open to homeschooled students. The IAHE maintains a list of many of these teams on our website: iahe.net/homeschool-sports

What About Access to Public School Programs?

Question:

What is the law regarding a homeschooled student's access to high school sports programs?

Answer:

Access to public sports programs is not a legal issue. Access to school sports programs is governed by the Indiana High School Athletic Association (IHSAA). Indiana homeschooled students are defined as non-public, non-accredited students and must meet the eligibility guidelines as in section 12-5 of the IHSAA By-Laws.

Question:

What does that mean for my family?

Answer:

Simply stated, each school district has the authority to establish their own rules and standards on what a student must do in order to participate in their sports programs. Over the past couple of years the IAHE has seen an increase in the requirements that school districts are putting on homeschooled families. It is up to each family to decide if they are willing to meet the guidelines put in place in order to participate.

Are you a homeschool family, providing a parent-directed, home-based, privately-funded education, and you have a student taking a class at the public school in order to play a sport? We are seeing an increase in the conditions placed on homeschool families. If you have been asked by the school to take the ISTEP, or another standardized test, please contact the IAHE first.

What About Academics and Socialization?

Dr. Brian Ray, president of the National Home Education Research Institute, states that, "The tutorial method has always been the superior method for educating children. Homeschooling epitomizes this method, providing the essentials for success: a close relationship between student and teacher, motivation, flexibility, and individualization."

Dr. Ray demonstrates in his research through a thorough evaluation of many national research studies that home educated students generally out-perform academically, emotionally, and socially those students who have been educated in the more traditional settings. His research shows that home educated children perform in the 80th percentile on nationally normed achievement tests. Dr. Ray's book, "Home Educated and Now Adults" give the history of the first 25 years of the modern homeschool movement as well as statistics which show what the home educated have accomplished.

Although the question, "What about socialization?" is one of the most commonly asked questions, home educated children typically get plenty of socialization through church and neighborhood friends, support group activities, co-op education classes, organized sports clubs and family members. It is unrealistic to think that spending large quantities of time with children their own age guarantees quality socialization for children, when, in fact, it can produce peer dependency and low self esteem. Many families have chosen to homeschool because they have seen the results of home education – self confident children with independent thinking skills, strong family roots and the ability to relate to people of all ages.

The **National Center for Home Education (NCHE)**, a division of **Home School Legal Defense Association (HSLDA)** released a study in 2003 titled 'Homeschooling Grows Up.' Conducted by Dr. Brian Ray of the **National Home Education Research Institute (NHERI)** and commissioned by HSLDA, the study answers homeschool skeptics who claim that homeschooling leads to poor socialization.

"Homeschool graduates are proving the critics wrong in every arena," said Tom Washburne, Director of NCHE. Every homeschool family has confronted the question "Oh, you homeschool. What about your child's socialization?" This study demonstrates that concerns about socialization are unfounded. Homeschoolers educated in the 1980's are coming of age and taking their place in society. In particular, the study found that homeschoolers are significantly more involved in their communities than the average public school graduate. Over 71% of homeschoolers participate in a voluntary, church or neighborhood association compared with 37% of U.S. adults. Over 76% of 18-24 homeschool graduates voted in a national/state election the past 5 years compared with just 29% of 18-24 year old public school graduates. "Homeschoolers, typically identified as high academic achievers, are doing well as adults in society," said Ray.

How Does My Student Get a Work Permit?

What Are the Requirements for Children Who Are Seeking Employment and Want to Work During Traditional School Hours?

Indiana law states that all minors ages 14-17, regardless of their attendance in public school, are required to obtain a work permit prior to any work or training. Work permits are obtained from the accredited high school in the district where the student resides.

Please see the Child Labor FAQs on the **Indiana Department of Labor** website for more information on how your child may obtain a work permit.

Homeschooled students are subject to the same hour and occupation restrictions as a traditional student. The work hour regulations can also be found on the Indiana Department of Labor website.

According to the Department of Labor, "a homeschool student may work during traditional school hours if he/she has written permission from a parent or homeschool tutor. This permission must be delivered in writing and should specify what hours the minor may work."

If your homeschooled child is having difficulty obtaining a work permit, you may contact the IAHE.

How Does My Student Get Their Driver's License?

Since many Indiana home educators teach their students to drive, here is helpful information regarding the process. Be sure to check out the most current information on the www.in.gov website.

Indiana Bmv Learner's Permit

You must be 16 to get your learner's permit in Indiana, if you are not enrolled in a paid driver's ed class endorsed by the State.

What Documentation Do We Need?

Student's birth certificate (original or certified counts as Identity & Lawful Status), and Social Security Card OR Paystub with the youth's SSN.

FINAL REQUIREMENT: Your BMV agent may **or** may not consider mail in your child's name acceptable to establish Indiana residency. The best way to be prepared & not need to make another trip is to bring all of the Secure ID Documents for your own self (birth certificate, driver's license, 2 pieces of mail in your name & to your address: bank statement and/or utility statements from past 60 days, your Social Security card & you will sign an affidavit for your child.

*Written Test & Vision Test are to be taken BEFORE obtaining a learner's permit.

What About Children with Special Needs?

Homeschooling can be the best alternative to meet the needs of the special needs child. There are excellent Christian books available on this topic and several organizations that help parents get the resources they need to educate their special needs child. Families of special needs children enjoy the same rights and freedoms as all other families in making choices for their children, but because special needs children are often more involved with the public school and "special services", it is recommended that parents of special needs children join Home School Legal Defense Association for any additional advice and counsel.

The IAHE is affiliated with JoyQuest. JoyQuest is an Indiana organization established to minister to parents of children with special needs.

The IAHE also maintains a full list of resources on our website for families seeking additional helps:

iahe.net/exploring-home-education/homeschooling-child-special-needs

What About Discounts for Homeschool Families?

Did you know?

Many companies offer educator discounts for teachers. As a home educator you can take advantage of the savings too! Registered users on the IAHE website can print a Teacher ID card.

Discounts and program qualifications vary and are subject to change. Visit the company's website for information about their current discount program.

Bookstore Discounts for Teachers

- Barnes & Noble
- Book Warehouse
- Books-a-Million
- Half Price Books

Retail Store Discounts for Teachers

- The Container Store
- FedEx Office Store
- Hancock Fabrics
- Home Depot
- JoAnn Fabrics
- Michaels
- Office Depot/Office Max
- Staples

Tech/Software Discounts for Teachers

- Adobe
- Apple Store
- Dell Computers
- Hewlett-Packard
- JourneyEd
- PBS Store

What About High School?

What About High School?

Many families find great joy in continuing their child's education through high school at home. Because coursework is done for credit, and credits are needed for graduation, there are some special considerations in planning a student's high school education.

Thousands of young people throughout the United States are graduating from home schools each year. Many are going on to college, some are going straight to the work force, some are joining the military, and some are starting their own businesses. What the statistics have shown is that the majority of home educated graduates are successfully moving into adulthood.

We now have had those who have gone before, who have successfully graduated young men and women from homeschooling. Those who are reaching this new level, can now move forward with less fear and more confidence, that they too can succeed. If God has placed this desire in your heart, may you move forward and graduate sons and daughters prepared for adulthood.

Why Homeschool Through High School

Dr. Jay Wile

When parents begin homeschooling their young children, they often say something like, "We'll do this for a few years and then send them to school when they get older." It sounds like a good idea. Give them a solid foundation in the elementary and perhaps even the junior high school years, and then send them off to a high school where expert teachers can prepare them for university or the workforce.

After all, while untrained parents can probably teach their children the basics, there is just no way to teach trigonometry, chemistry, and creative writing without specialized training. Since most parents don't have enough specialized training to teach such higher-level subjects, it only makes sense that at some point, homeschooling won't be the best option for them.

It only makes sense, *but it is almost certainly wrong.* Several studies show that students who graduate from homeschool and then go on to pursue a college education are significantly more successful than their peers who went to public or private school. For example, a study from the University of St. Thomas indicates that students who were homeschooled in high school had higher grade point averages and a significantly higher four-year graduation rate than those who went to public or private high schools. Other universities, such as Boston University, Kennesaw State University, and Baylor University, report similar results.

Why do students who were homeschooled in high school do better at college than those who go to school? There are probably several reasons, but I think the main one has to do with the peer group. When children are young, the peer group has some influence on their behavior, but the older they get, the more important its influence becomes. Of course, the peer group isn't very wise. It rarely values hard work, good grades, and delayed gratification. As a result, students who go to school in their high school years are being strongly influenced to avoid those things that will make them successful later in life.

The peer group also tends to make students less sensitive to the things that really matter. It emphasizes material things over spiritual things. As a result, students tend to ignore what's important in an attempt to chase after short-term gratification. This, of course, can lead to some very bad consequences.

My father used to be the assistant superintendent at one of Indiana's maximum-security prisons. He was in charge of assimilating new inmates into the prison. As a part of what he did, he asked each inmate a series of questions. Some were mandated by the state, and some he made up himself. One of his questions was, "If you could tell your parents one thing they should have done differently while raising you, what would it be?" He says that the vast majority of his inmates answered with something like, "Monitor my friends more carefully." The older the student gets, the more important it is to monitor the peer group, and that is best done at home.

While this an important reason to homeschool through high school, there are many others as well. However, I think the best reason to homeschool through high school was given by a homeschool graduate. Her name is Naomi, and she currently runs her own business, which grew out of a homeschool assignment her father gave her. She says, "Thinking back, I love that every childhood memory I have is at home with my family...I have lived a homeschooled life; and what a joy it has been. I consider myself very blessed."

Honestly, I envy Naomi. I have a many childhood memories and teen memories that are associated with a lot of people I don't really care for, because they involve things that happened at school. If you want to prepare your children as best you can for their future while making memories that are filled with family and love, you should homeschool them all the way through high school.

Dr. Jay L. Wile holds an earned Ph.D. in nuclear chemistry and a B.S. in chemistry, both from the University of Rochester. He has won several awards for excellence in teaching and has presented lectures on the topics of Nuclear Chemistry, Christian Apologetics, Homeschooling, and Creation vs. Evolution. He is best known for his award-winning "Exploring Creation With..." series of science textbooks. Dr. Wile and his wife of more than 25 years, Kathleen, homeschooled their daughter, Dawn, from the time they adopted her until she graduated high school. Dawn is a Butler University graduate and is currently a long-haul trucker with her husband, James. Visit Dr. Wile on the web at http://www.drwile.com.

The Key to Motivating Teens:
Learning in the Context of Life and Truth

Dr. and Mrs. Ronald Jay (Inge) Cannon, Education PLUS

Think back to your school years as a child or a teen. What lessons were most efficiently learned - the ones you gleaned from a textbook in response to a scheduled assignment or the ones where you were desperate to find the answers to a problem you needed to solve at work, at home, at church, or in your own personal life? If you're like most people, you'll have to admit that most of the assignments were important, but the lessons you learned in the context of your need to know, offered skills with "staying power."

We are living in a time when the technology around us makes learning "in context of need" ever more possible. Today's students have access to electronic tools, which literally put the world at the touch of a remote control. Learning at home is becoming more practical by the minute.

It is also becoming more crucial. Parental responsibility to train young people in discernment is heightened by the cyberspace revolution. Discernment is a function of wisdom, and wisdom - the ability to understand from God's perspective - comes only by immersion in God's Word.

In his thought-provoking book School's Out, author Lewis Perelman predicts that the knowledge explosion produced by the technological revolution of the late twentieth century is rapidly producing a world in which memorization of facts will have to take a back seat to learning how to find and interpret the information one needs. He explains, "The data storage technology of the next century will put a lifetime of information in the palm of your hand. Long before that, however, the measure of human competence in the [hyper learning] world will be not what you can remember, but what you can understand.

Dr. Perelman prophesies that "distance learning" and "telecourses" will "erode the foundation of academic bureaucracies in much the same ways they are topping the established institutional structures of the telephone, broadcast television, and financial services industries." He envisions schools that are "not identified with any distinct building of location, but rather with a brand or franchise of media through which services are accessed. Home technology - video, audio, computer, and telephone - is far more adroit at meeting diverse life cycle needs for entertainment, information, work, and learning than is the technology of conventional academic structures. And telelearning technology can help converse the modem family's scarcest resource, time."

Dr. Perelman's advice to individual families is to become "school proof." Begin by participating in the kind of political action, which will reinforce change because the current situation is costing every taxpayer a fortune. Create a home where learning is a necessary part of your way of life in the sense of a normal, daily activity for the whole family. "Children become what they behold. Parents who are learners have children who are learners. "

Focus on learning "in context" because the most valuable learning takes place, not in classrooms, but in doing real things in real places connected with real people in real social institutions .... " This kind of learning labeled "Just in Time" or JIT learning - is so efficient that Dr. Peleman urges families wherever possible to homeschool. He believes that home educators have the unique opportunity to live on the cutting edge of education.

But there is one more dimension to the cyberspace revolution-that is, a desperate urgency for Christian parents to teach their young people discernment. When you live in a world where everything has the potential of being viewed on your personal computer screen, it becomes even more crucial to be able to "try the spirits," so that only what is good will be kept in the heart and mind. Discernment is a function of wisdom, the ability to understand from God's perspective which comes only by immersing ourselves in the Scripture. It is far better to learn less in terms of encyclopedic knowledge and be able to use effectively what we have learned to further God's Kingdom while we are on earth. From that vantage point, we describe the unique possibilities that discipleship of teens in the homeschool can offer.

What Does the World Expect Us to Know?

High school diplomas are generally awarded in the United States to students who earn a minimum of 16-20 Carnegie units. A Carnegie unit is the educational measurement which represents time spent in a course of study, usually 36 weeks, 5 days per week, 45-50 minutes per class hour.

Most conventional credentials include the following:

3-4 units of English

Possibilities include literary genres (general survey), American literature, British literature, world literature and philosophy. Elective areas may add journalism, creative writing, or literacy criticism. (Note: Grammar & composition are generally studied each year related to the literary components.)

2-3 units of Mathematics

Possibilities include consumer math, two years of algebra, geometry, trigonometry, and calculus.

1-2 units of Science

Possibilities include biology (specifically required for graduation in many states), general science, physics, and chemistry. Advanced studies may include anatomy, microbiology, and detailed projects in botany, zoology, astronomy, or biochemistry.

2 units of History

Possibilities include U.S. history (required for graduation in many states), world history, world geography, government and economics. (Note: Students in conventional schools generally must pass an extensive examination demonstrating knowledge of the U.S. Constitution.)

2 units of Physical Education

These usually earn credit at the rate a ½ unit per year, and classroom work in health, hygiene, driver education, and career orientation is often included a part of the course of study.

1 unit of Fine Arts

Performance courses are often considered 'minor' in the curriculum and therefore also earn credit at the rate of Y2 units per year. This designation allows for the fact the classroom time is spent in practice to perfect skills rather than in direct instruction as in 'major' courses.

3 units of Electives

Possibilities include foreign language study (two year sequence recommended for entrance into some fields of college or graduate study), business education (typing, shorthand, general office skills, bookkeeping, basic accounting), computer science, vocational courses (various shops and apprenticeships), and home economics (nutrition and food preparation, sewing and tailoring, home decorations, and home management).Christian schools usually add a Bible requirement comprising of one year of study for each term in attendance.

What Does God Want Us to Know?

When exploring God's requirements for what our young people learn, it is important to establish a scriptural definition of knowledge. II Peter 1: 5-8 provides a clear description for an educational sequence which will honor God: "Add to your faith virtue; and to virtue knowledge; and to knowledge temperance; and to temperance patience; and to patience godliness; and to godliness brotherly kindness; and to brotherly kindness charity. For if these things be in you and abound, they make you that ye shall neither be barren nor unfruitful in the knowledge of our Lord Jesus Christ."

Knowledge then is explored information within the boundaries of faith and character development. There are some things God commands His children not to know. He told Adam and Eve that they were not to know evil (Genesis 2: 17), and the Apostle Paul affirmed this instruction to the Roman Christians when he wrote, "1 would have you wise unto that which is good, and simple concerning evil" (Romans 16: 19b).

Learning the true meaning of knowledge requires a wise and understanding heart, which is developed when students allow wisdom to teach them through life's experiences. The book of Proverbs makes this strong appeal. Reasoning skills are strengthened as analogies are used to identify relationships. Many spiritual truths are developed through analogs, and Jesus often used this means of teaching His disciples.

Each subject matter area that comes under consideration in a Christian home school should be examined in light of scriptural directives. The following list is broader than a mere high school credential; it seeks to define the 'end product' of an educational program as scripture would affirm the goals. These are mastery areas young people should accomplish sometime during their preparation for adulthood.

Regarding communication skills, God's Word commands that "we minister grace to the hearers..." with our words (Ephesians 4:29). We are reminded as well that we will "Give account for every idle word ..." (Matthew 12:36), and that our words must be precise in sending forth a clear signal. Thus, we know that students should master grammar and syntax, the ability to express themselves with the written and spoken word, to be persuasive and instructive or encouraging as situations demand. Because technology enhances our ability to produce the written word, every student should master computer/typewriter/keyboard skills.

Where does the realm of literature fit in? Familiarity with great writings will help a student internalize excellent, descriptive means of expressing himself. Many people ask, "What is a classic?" A work that has stood the test of time and is true to Biblical themes in dealing accurately with life's challenges is an excellent threshold point for evaluation. He who walks with great men will become wise. Reading is the most accessible and powerful means we have to allow students the consistent company of great individuals.

Scripture explicitly commands that we know history: "For whatsoever things were written aforetime were written for our learning, that we … might have hope" (Romans 15:4). We gain hope or confidence as we learn how God operates His universe and understand His ways in dealing with mankind. Because history is really "His Story," it should begin with the Scripture-the Old Testament.

Israel's history offers a clear demonstration of when people experience blessings and when they experienced cursing. "Blessed is the nation whose God is the Lord," the Psalmist reminds us (Psalms 33: 12). Against this backdrop, study the rise and fall of each civilization according to the pattern of Israel's relationship with Jehovah. Then examine U.S. history in light of that same pattern. Such an approach gives context and understanding (developing wisdom) to the study and removes the student from the dreadful futility of memorizing meaningless fact.

The next logical place to move a scriptural oriented educational credential is church history. How is God dealing with man during this present age? Begin with Acts, move through the epistles (examining, of course, the times and places where these churches were located), and culminate the study by relating the seven churches referenced in Revelation to the major periods in church history. Current events should be correlated to scripture, and the development of missions must be explored in this context (forming a meaningful basis for the study of geography). The final phase of understanding plumbs the depths of prophecy.

The prophet Isaiah described the three-branch structure of government long before Christ was born: "For the Lord is our Judge, The Lord is our lawgiver, the Lord is our King; He will save us" (Isaiah 33:22). As you study government, examine the U.S. Constitution point-by point relationship to Biblical principles or foundational references.

That "He is before all things … by Him all things consist" (Colossians 1: 17) forms the rationale and protective framework for the study of science. Honor the limitations of science by formulating a precise definition. Then create a study from hypothesis to evaluation. Understand how thinking with analogies enhances creativity in inventions. Skill in taxonomy will promote understanding of the orderliness of God's creation and build a foundation for an effective apologetic refuting evolutionary thinking.

The primary use of mathematics, which is corroborated in scripture, is accurate business dealings. "A false balance is abomination to the Lord, but a just weight is his delight" (Proverbs 11: 1). Character development and reputation (a 'good name ') is inextricably tied to a person's application of proper stewardship. In conventional curriculum, the scientific expressions of higher mathematics often preclude consumer and business math. The development of the 'higher' skills is by no means wrong; in fact, it is an expression of an exact science. But responsibility in a man's business and home must not be ignored to make room for trigonometry and calculus.

God promised to make his people "the head and not the tail..." (Deuteronomy 28: 13) if they would honor His principles in matters of borrowing, lending, and investing. Young people must learn how the "borrower" becomes "servant to the lender" (Proverbs 22: 7), and cause/effect relationships regarding debt and prosperity need to be carefully analyzed.

Art and music are the language of the spirit. God gave mankind these means of glorifying His name. The Psalmist describes a heart that is right with God through a musical analogy: "He hath put a new song in my mouth, even praise unto our God; many shall see it and fear and shall trust in the Lord" (Psalm 40: 3). The standard for what to study and what to produce is defined in Philippians 4:8: "Whatsoever things are true ... honest ... just ... pure .. .lovely ... of good report; If there be any virtue, and if there be any praise, think on these things." We honor God when the expressions of our hearts and our being are consistent with His character. Therefore, any study of the arts must be limited to those means and expressions which draw the believer closer to becoming Christ like and demonstrate God's character to a world that doesn't know Him. Young people must develop their gifts so that they are not merely consumers of the arts, but producers of excellence.

Finally, don't forget to teach your young ladies how to be "keepers at home" (see Titus 2: 4-5 and Proverbs 31) and equip your young men to support their own households (see I Timothy 5: 8 and Proverbs 24: 27). Honoring your son's or daughter's individual bent and following God's direction will round out the picture, allowing you to craft your program to God's design for your family.

The 1828 American Directory of the English Language by Noah Webster earmarks four necessary components in every person's education: Education comprehends all that series of instruction and discipline which is intended to enlighten the understanding, correct the temper, and form the manners and habits of youth, and fit them for usefulness in their future stations." Such an education demands earning more than a list of credits; it demands mature understanding of God's precepts as they impact every subject.

Dr. and Mrs. Ronald Jay (Inge) Cannon are the owners of Education Plus+. Mrs. Cannon is a speaks at home-school functions, she is the author of materials that aid in training your children, especially teens. Used with permission.

High School Transcripts: A Simple Checklist

Inge Cannon

Putting together an official transcript for your homeschooled highschooler can seem like an overwhelming task. But this is one area where out-of-the-box homeschoolers need to make themselves intelligible within the system. Inge Cannon, executive director of Education PLUS, lends her expertise as homeschoolers tackle the transcript.

DON'T even think about not providing your children with high school transcripts! No matter where a student is educated—public school, private school, or homeschool—that student deserves a transcript from the people who organized the academic program, taught the courses, and evaluated the work. If you want to teach high schoolers at home, you absolutely must provide them with the documentation of a transcript.

DO grant your children a high school diploma. High school graduation is an important benchmark and transition point in a young person's life, and it should be honored as such. Your children deserve the right to say "yes" on job applications that ask if they have a high school diploma!

DON'T use the GED to document high school graduation. You may find yourself in situations that require a GED test score for screening or admissions purposes (however unjustified by law), but that does not mean you have to document graduation by a method that often carries the stigma of a high school dropout.

DO identify each child thoroughly on his or her transcript. You will need to indicate full legal name, current address, gender, birth date, parent or legal guardian name(s), and a Social Security number (especially crucial if you are applying for any financial aid to go to college).

DON'T feel obligated to make your transcripts match the public school system in timeline, structure, sequence, curricular options, or anything else. Home education is a tutorial process; thus, it is important to focus on the needs, interests, talents, and gifts of each individual child. Most tutorial education procedures do not follow the typical school structure of living between classroom bells and being classified as freshman, sophomore, junior, or senior—let alone sitting in lecture sessions of designated length and completing routine "busywork" assignments.

DO limit yourself to two pages (or one sheet front and back) for your printed transcript. Transcripts (like resumés) are supposed to present a summary of achievement and/or experience—short enough for the reader to know at a glance who the student is and what he has done. In academic and most employment circles, anything more than two pages becomes a portfolio.

DON'T succumb to any pressure— real or imagined—to require a college preparatory course lineup in order to graduate your children from high school. You do not have to satisfy any college admissions requirements to earn a high school diploma (i.e., there is absolutely nothing wrong with a diploma focused on apprenticeship, the trades, the arts, or any other pursuit of knowledge and skills). However, it does make sense if your child is college-bound to work the college's admissions requirements into the student's high school preparation.

DO use your child's transcripts as an annual report card. This is especially helpful when applying for good driver discounts on auto insurance and work permits when employers need them, or to accompany resumés or applications for volunteer and paid positions, etc.

DON'T skip physical education credits. Some colleges actually ask students to make up deficiencies in physical education when they enroll. Remember that physical education generally earns half the credit that would be earned for a comparable amount of academic work.

DO include Bible credits if yours is a Christian program. Even if a college tells you that it does not recognize "Bible" or "Religious Studies," your transcript should not be crafted by what the college accepts or denies. The transcript is a report of the work your child has completed.

DON'T be rigid about counting hours when assigning Carnegie Units. There is a great deal of variety in the computation of hours required to earn a Carnegie Unit of credit— requirements as low as 120 all the way to 250 hours! Since home education involves a tutorial process of teaching and learning, you will find many occasions when your child's academic achievement is difficult to document in terms of a specific number of hours. Some situations work best with documentation by textbook equivalency, while others should have a diary of work experiences coupled with a bibliography for training. The important thing is that you know why you assigned a specific amount of credit to a course and that any variation from course to course reflects your stated objectives (and yes, for this you do need to do some planning!).

DO be consistent in your assignment of credits and grades—this is no place for emotional entanglement! Teachers do not give students grades. Students earn grades, and teachers simply record them accurately and honestly. Remember that consistency and equality are not synonyms—an A in math will be documented with different criteria than an A in Public Speaking, Home Economics, Orchestra, or World History. Planning your objectives for learning will help you make strategic assignments and identify the levels of achievement that deserve an A, B, C, and so on.

DON'T "weight" grades with extra GPA points unless you have the proper documentation for doing so. "Weighting" refers to a process of adding an extra grade point to a grade when the coursework is advanced (i.e., Advanced Placement or AP, college courses completed during the high school years, and Honors courses where you have a detailed syllabus that outlines the extra work requirements).

DO include the necessary statistical summaries: Grade Point Average (GPA) and a tally of the number of credits per subject área (e.g., Math, Foreign Language, English, Fine Arts, Social Sciences, Natural Sciences, Physical Education, etc.). While the most common GPA system involves a 4-point scale, there are at least four other possibilities for making this crucial college admissions calculation. Do a little research about what is common in your state, and then use the same system for the entire transcript. Remember that "class rank" should not be included—after all, your child is number one in a class of one!

DON'T forget standardized achievement test scores. DO report only the National Percentile Rank and Stanine (NPR/S), and avoid listing any grade equivalents. DO skip the subtest reports and work with the major sections of the assessment (i.e., Mathematics, Reading Comprehension or Language Arts, Basic Battery or Complete Battery).

DO include at least a summary of SAT and/or ACT scores—even though each college admissions officer will want a score report sent directly from the test provider.

DO figure out what addendum sheets should be attached to each program. Possibilities include Bibliography of Text Resources, Course Descriptions, Special Features of a Student's Program, Method of Computing GPA, Guidance Counselor Recommendations, Work in Progress: Senior Year, Extracurricular Activity Descriptions, and so forth.

DON'T omit a specific high school graduation date—even if you have to list a projected date for juniors who submit early applications to colleges.

DO sign your child's transcripts and provide a contact telephone number and/or e-mail address. While an embossed seal can add the "aura of officialness," it is not required.

Inge Cannon has served the homeschool movement for almost 25 years and is currently the executive director of Education PLUS. She is the author/seminar instructor of Transcript Boot Camp on DVD. Her TranscriptPro software gives the professional edge to every parent and is extremely easy to use. Details are available at www.homeschooltranscripts.com *and* www.edplus.com

Uniquely Indiana

minnetrista.net

Top Educational Attractions in Indiana

All information is subject to change.

Prices, discounts, and reciprocal agreements listed are from Fall 2015.

1. Organization: Benjamin Harrison Presidential Site

Family Basic Membership: $50

General Admission: $10 adult; $9 ages 65+, $5 ages 5-17

Current Discounts Available: $5 off new membership if you have a current membership to certain organizations.

Homeschool Day/Discounts: Third Thursday of the month. Field trips are also offered at a discount rate.

2.) Organization: Children's Museum of Indianapolis

Family Basic Membership: $159

General Admission: $21.50 adult; $18.50 ages 2-17; $20.50 ages 60+; Access Pass $1

3.) Organization: Conner Prairie

Family Basic Membership: $90

General Admission: Admission varies based on season.

Reciprocal: Smithsonian affiliate and Time Travelers Affiliate

4.) Organization: Creation Museum (near Cincinnati)

Family Basic Membership: $178

General Admission: $29.95 adult; $23.95 ages 60+; $15.95 ages 5-12. Online coupons available.

Current Discounts Available: $5 off for homeschoolers with membership to HSLDA and other organizations.

5. Organization: Eiteljorg

Family Basic Membership: $65

Educator Cost; any additional stipulations, i.e. min students: ALL Indiana teachers (K-12) with ID proof of current school employment.

Reciprocal: Time Travelers program

6. Organization: Classical Music Indy (formerly Fine Arts Society)

7. Organization: Fort Wayne Zoo

Family Basic Membership: $109

General Admission: $14 adult; $9 ages 2-18; $10.50 ages 60+

Reciprocal: Yes! Reciprocal to other zoos listed here. Good for discounted admission.

Homeschool Day/Discounts:

8. Organization: Indiana Historical Society

Family Basic Membership: $75

General Admission: $7 adults; $5 ages 5-17; 0-4 free; 60+ $6.50

Reciprocal: Time Travelers program

Homeschool Day/Discounts: Discounted Field Trip rate on website

9. Organization: Indiana Landmarks

Family Basic Membership: Varies

10. Organization: Indianapolis Art Center

Family Basic Membership: Varies

11. Organization: Indianapolis Museum of Art

Family Basic Membership: $75

Reciprocal: Reciprocal for Advocate level members

12. Organization: Indianapolis Zoo

Family Basic Membership: $136

General Admission: Admission varies based on season.

13. Organization: Indiana State Museum

Family Basic Membership: $72

Educator Cost; any additional stipulations, i.e. min students: All Indiana K-12 teachers receive free admission to the Indiana State Museum year round with valid school identification.

General Admission: Adults $13; Seniors $12; Students $8.50. Access Pass

Current Discounts Available: Save $5 off membership if you already have a membership to certain museums listed here: Indianapolis Zoo, Conner Prairie, Indianapolis Museum of Art, Indiana Historical Society, Eiteljorg, Indiana Landmarks, Fine Arts Society, Classical 88.7, Indianapolis Art Center, and Benjamin Harrison Presidential Site.

14. Organization: Indiana State Parks and Reservoir

Family Basic Membership: $99-199 depending on package.

Educator Cost; any additional stipulations, i.e. min students:

General Admission:

15. Organization: Muncie Children's Museum

Family Basic Membership: $70

Educator Cost; any additional stipulations, i.e. min students:

General Admission: $6 per person ages 1-100. Printable coupons available.

16. Organization: Science Central, Fort Wayne

17. Organization: Wonderlab Museum, Bloomington

18. Organization: Corydon Capitol State Historic Site, Corydon

General Admission: Adults - $5, Children - $2

Current Discounts Available: Special rates are available for groups of 10 or more and for school groups.

Reciprocal: Indiana State Museum members receive FREE admission.

Historic Corydon and the Harrison County Visitor's Bureau are a valued Informer magazine advertiser.

19. Organization: Gene Stratton-Porter State Historic Site, Rome City

General Admission: Adults -$,Students: $2

Reciprocal: Indiana State Museum members receive FREE admission and a 10 percent discount in the gift shop.

School Groups: Special rates are available for groups of 10 or more and for school groups.

20. Organization: Minnetrista, Muncie

General Admission: $5

Minnetrista offers a variety of multi-disciplinary school tours for Grades Pre-K through 8. These programs are active and engaging, while also standards-based and content-rich for your educational demands.

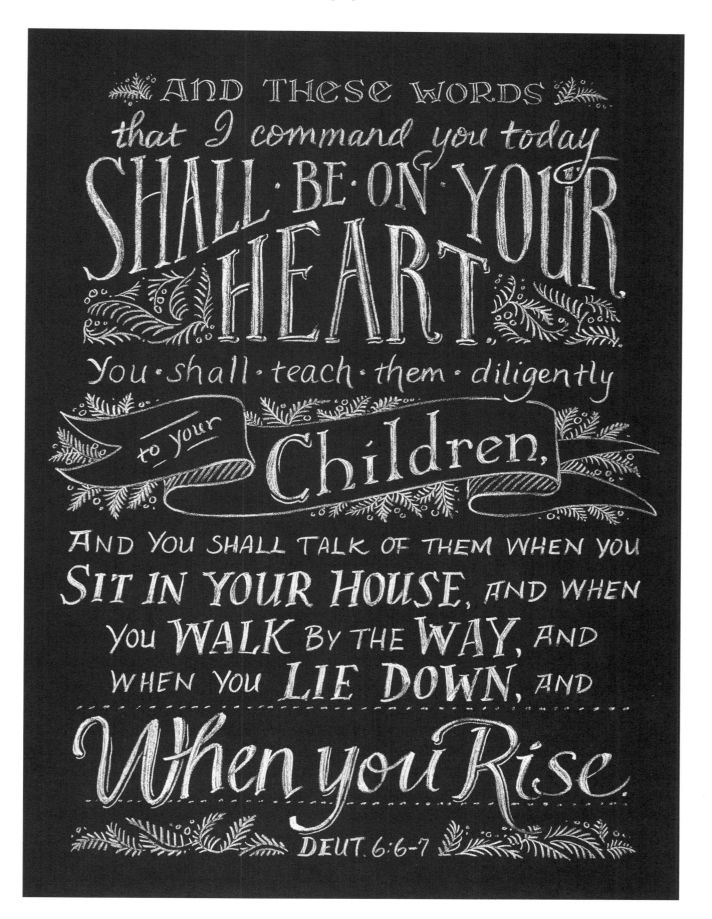

Encouragement for the Journey

How Will I Ever Get It All Done?

Mary Carney

If you're new to homeschooling (or even if you're not,) the demands of your children's academic education on top of housework and cooking can be overwhelming. Sixteen years ago, when we started our homeschool adventure, I was totally unprepared for the workload. In the intervening years, we've graduated our two oldest from high school, assisted them in the launch to college and careers, and learned a thing or two about streamlining and organizing. This comes in handy as we still have two grade-schoolers at home.

I offer you here my TOP TEN LIST of things you can do to get a handle on your homemaking responsibilities while homeschooling. (With apologies to David Letterman!)

#10 SPEND A WEEK ON HOME ECONOMICS

We always spend the first week of school on Home Ec. We de-junk, weed out closets and catch up on all those little projects we didn't get to over the summer. If you can afford it, hire someone to do the 'scrubby-cleany' stuff while you sort, organize, and clear out clutter. Eat simple meals off of paper plates, cancel all non-essential outings for the week, and try to get the most important stuff done.

#9 AUTOMATE YOUR WEEKDAY BREAKFAST AND LUNCH ROUTINES.

Nothing deflates a day of learning like spending half an hour trying to decide what to have for lunch. We have a regular schedule of breakfasts and lunches (yes, it's written down!) Not only is it easier on the brain, but it makes it much simpler to work in those important servings of fruits and vegetables and whole grains.

#8 SCHEDULE A COOKING DAY.

Choose four meals which your family likes and which freeze well, such as spaghetti sauce, meatloaf, and such. Make a quadruple batch of each and your diners for half of next month are already taken care of. This really takes the pressure off on hectic days.

#7 ARRANGE A PLANNING DAY AWAY FROM HOME WITH YOUR SPOUSE.

Use this time to set goals for the year, review curriculum choices, and articulate your reasons for homeschooling. Pray for each other, your children, your support group, and the IAHE and it's leadership. Even if you just spend a couple of hours at a picnic table in the park, step back for a few hours to contemplate God's Will for your family.

#6 CAST A VERY CRITICAL EYE ON OUTSIDE ACTIVITIES.

Remember that saying "yes" to an activity means saying "no" to something else. Have the strength to say "no" when appropriate. Trust me, your children will not turn out to be hopeless, socially backwards geeks if you don't sign up for every activity and class your support group offers.

#5 TEACH EVERY CHILD ONE NEW CHORE SKILL PER MONTH.

Delegate after training is complete; remember to follow-up and inspect. You will find your children can do much more than you ever thought if you only give them a chance.

#4 SPEND TEN MINUTES BEFORE YOU GO TO BED GETTING READY FOR TOMORROW.

Set out the skillet for breakfast, set the table, put to thaw in the frig tomorrow's dinner, and lay out clothing for younger children. Nothing slows you down in the morning like waking up to yesterday's work!

#3 ESTABLISH CONSISTENT TIMES FOR WAKING, SLEEPING, AND MEALS.

It is especially important for you, Mom, to get a good night's sleep. The world will go on turning even if you miss the eleven o'clock news!

#2 UNPLUG YOUR TV AND COMPUTER.

Up until a few years ago, we all lived without e-mail (I still do!) I know more than a few folks who wouldn't dream of spending three or four hours a day watching TV, but devote that and more to e-mail and other forms of cyber-entertainment. We lived totally without TV for over seven yeas, and it was the best seven years ever. Try it!

#1 BUY A NEW BOX OF CRAYONS.

Ok, this won't go a long way towards an efficient, organized home. But go on, splurge and get the jumbo, deluxe 120 crayon assortment. There's nothing like that new crayon smell to let you know this will be the best school year yet!

Mary Carney has been married 38 years. She is the mother of four- ages 18-33, grandmother of one, recently retired after 25 years of homeschooling. Pediatric ICU RN, nurse researcher.

Tomorrow is Always Fresh, with No Mistakes

Rebecca Scarlata Keliher

I'll start Monday. Yes, Monday is a good day to start things anew. It is the best time to start a new diet or a new routine for exercise, better eating, or early morning devotions. Best of all, Monday is the day I will, once again, dive into my planner and set a course for the "perfect" homeschool day. My children will delightfully acknowledge and properly respond to my wishes, yes, on Monday. For today it is Tuesday, and so I will start next Monday.

Have you ever had that conversation with yourself? Best intentions in mind, you start out on Monday and by the very next day things have already fallen out of sorts and you are justifying why you should wait until the following Monday to start anew?

As a young mother of three little girls, our home would not have been complete without all three VHS videos of Anne of Green Gables. Tea party table set up, delicate cookies to snack on, and dressed up like princesses, the girls and I would spend the afternoon on Prince Edward Island.

I'll never forget the moment I heard the statement from Ms. Stacy, "Tomorrow is always fresh with no mistakes in it... well with no mistakes in it yet."

The thought had not occurred to me before. Tomorrow is always the best time to start anew, try it again, and give it another go. So why do we put off the tomorrow for the next Monday?

One of my favorite authors, Martin Lloyd Jones, a minister of the early twentieth century stated it best:

> *Have you realized that most of your unhappiness in life is due to the fact that you are listening to yourself instead of talking to yourself? Take those thoughts that come to you the moment you wake up in the morning. You have not originated them, but they start talking to you, they bring back the problems of yesterday, etc. Somebody is talking. Who is talking to you? Your self is talking to you. Now this man's treatment [the Psalmist in Psalm 42] was this; instead of allowing this self to talk to him, he starts talking to himself. 'Why art thou cast down, O my soul?' he asks. His soul has been depressing him, crushing him. So he stands up and says: 'Self, listen for a moment, I will speak to you.' Do you know what I mean? If you do not, you have had but little experience.*

Homeschooling is not for the faint of heart and even with the best intentions; our schedules and routines can end up in the ditch. What to do? **Tell yourself to start again tomorrow.** Yes, it's as simple as that.

Not sure how to start? Here's an easy yet effective tool that I have used as I have planned, failed, evaluated and then planned again.

Get out a pencil and a piece of paper. On the vertical, jot down the times of the day, from the moment your feet hit the floor until it's night time, in increments of 30 minutes. On the horizontal, begin outlining the most important parts of the day: meals! You've gotta feed the kiddos if you expect to have any type of order. Next, jot down any commitments outside the home like piano, soccer, baseball, drama, co-op, etc.

You are almost ready to schedule in the homeschooling but first, stop for a moment and just stare. Stare hard and let it sink in, asking yourself this important question: Am I overscheduling myself **before** adding our schooling to the schedule?

As homeschooling has become mainstream, it has also become more convoluted with a plethora of available activities. Socialization, exercise, and outings are important and have their place, but the primary purpose of education is... drum roll please, you don't want to miss it... **education**. That's right, if you are homeschooling, it's pretty important to actually school the kids.

Ok, I am now stepping off my soapbox and back to that pencil and paper. Getting back to the horizontal, begin assigning the most difficult and time consuming subjects first then proceed to the remaining subjects. Remember to leave room for breaks and cuddling time over a good book on the couch.

The next morning, **your tomorrow**, post the schedule on the refrigerator and give it a try. As you go, you will see where adjustments can and should be made. It's not a big deal; your investment at this point is a piece of paper and a pencil. In the evening, get a fresh piece of paper, and try again, including your adjustments. Try again and in a few days, if needed, make a few more adjustments. Days turn into weeks, and weeks into months.

Children grow, schedules change and life throws you a curve ball every so often, but in the end, planning a successful day (ok, we'll try for a decent day) of homeschooling is as simple as a piece of paper, a pencil, and a tomorrow.

Rebecca Keliher, known as the "Well Planned Gal" is a homeschool mom who's passionate about the gospel, parenting, and an organized life. With over fifteen years of homeschooling experience, two graduated students, one married daughter, and a new grandchild, she loves sharing the many ups and downs of her journey. She hopes to walk alongside parents and let them know the wonderful opportunity for building relationships that homeschooling affords.

Homeschooling Without Co-op, Tutors, or Online Classes... Does it Work?

Susan Hoffman

The battle for the freedom to homeschool was fought by those who came before me. Their work to make homeschooling legal in our country and the steps they took to pave the way for others, have benefited those of us who follow; but as time went on, families have made different choices in the way they homeschool. Many choose to participate in co-ops or online classes, or hire a tutor. I made a different choice and homeschooled, at home.

As I am approaching the close of my homeschooling career, which began in 1996 and will end in May 2017, I recently received some good news. My youngest, as a first semester junior, received his ACT score. His composite score was 33. He had taken the PSAT as a sophomore, and did well, but we chose to forego the PSAT as a junior, and instead focus on the ACT, to minimize the number of tests so that he could maximize his time on other activities.

One reason we decided to forego the PSAT as a junior was because we were not interested in the work it takes to become a finalist, if he did score well enough to compete for that honor. Again, we were considering the cost of time, and the busy-ness to come: applying to colleges and writing essays, traveling for college visits, completing scholarship applications, and keeping up with his Civil Air Patrol duties and Tae Kwon Do training and teaching. Also, my oldest had taken the PSAT and earned a "Commended" ranking. In the end, it didn't matter; achieving the award of Finalist is a high honor, but it does not always translate into more scholarship money, as scholarship awards can be based on other factors such as available funding. My middle son's PSAT test was lost, and in the long run, it did not matter. So, instead of spending time preparing for the PSAT, my youngest planned to study for the ACT.

My older two did well on the ACT, scoring 33 and 32. They did well on the SAT, too. My oldest scored 800 on reading, 740 on writing, and 680 on math. My middle son scored 740, 670, and 670, respectively. None of the boys enrolled in test prep classes. For the older two, I bought the current year's test study book and they plowed through that as part of their daily school work. For my youngest, I bought nothing. He prepared by using the ACT website's study guides.

How did my boys' achieve their success? Did they have expert teachers? Attend local homeschool co-ops? Find online classes and tutors to nurture them along? No. They each worked hard, at the kitchen table, on their own. Homeschooling, without co-ops, online classes, or tutors produces independent learners who can achieve academic success and earn scholarships.

Taking to heart the adage that homeschooling is not public school at home, I didn't think it necessary to write lessons plans. Instead, my plan was to follow the old paths and to stand on the wise shoulders of those who came before me: I highly recommend to you my friends Harvey and Laurie Bluedorn of triviumpursuit.com. Their 1996 homeschooling seminar was the first I attended when I began my almost-complete journey of homeschooling.

What gave our homeschool the foundation for future success was Trivium Pursuit's article, "Ten Things to do with Your Child Before Age 10," These 10 things establish the foundation on which the later years build. These ten (reading, writing, narration, obedience, service, etc.) helped to establish discipline and order. Teaching to read and write was is time intensive, and training in obedience is a labor of love, but the resulting outcome of their attention to their studies, and their perseverance to complete them, has been effective. When expectations are laid out and established early, they become a habit and a routine which provides the momentum to continue.

Another recommendation of the Bluedorn's that I put into practice was little to no television. As a substitute, we did a couple of hours of reading aloud each day. As I look back, this was our favorite part of homeschooling. I think that we would have never done this had we participated in co-ops or online or outside classes. I did not choose computer learning, except for typing, until their high school years, when online research became a necessity. I also did not allow television. I believe the less screen time, the better.

One item not on the list to do before age 10 is formal math. I did not start textbook math with my younger two boys until they were almost 10. We then started Saxon 54 and both boys completed 54, 65, and 76, in two years. I had read about the value of delaying formal math from Trivium Pursuit. It saves time and difficulty to wait until the brain is more developed and able to handle abstract concepts (which is why there are so many manipulative type elementary math curriculae). Also, it then goes into the proper location in the brain, where it is more easily retrieved. For further information, I recommend this article I read years ago: "Research on the Teaching of Math, Formal Arithmetic at Age Ten, Hurried or Delayed?" by Harvey Bluedorn. If you do a search for "math" on the triviumpursuit.com website, you will find more recent posts.

Initially, in addition to learning Latin along with the older two, I would read aloud to them their daily history, science and math lessons. But when the youngest needed to be taught to read and write, I did not have time to do this and all my other duties as well, so the older two were then on their own. My middle son once complained that he thought he could learn better if he could just listen to his lessons instead of reading them. I apologized to him, and let him know that listening is a good way to learn, but reading is, too. Though he may have preferred to be an auditory learner, he transitioned successfully to learning visually. Eventually, both have to be mastered. In that regard, our schooling was more traditional. It was done at a desk or at the kitchen table. I did allow quiet play and art work during our read aloud times, but for traditional subjects, I don't agree with kinesthetic learning. In the past 5 or 6 years, I read an article in the WSJ reporting on a study that gave little value to learning styles, which confirmed my practice. The most memorable line from that review was that eventually, you cannot learn algebra by dancing.

One subject that I wish I had started earlier in my boys education and that I might add to the list of "10 things before age 10," was learning to play an instrument. The beauty of learning to play an instrument is that it does utilize all three learning pathways. However, there was only so much time in the day, and my days, and theirs, were full. Despite that lack, I am thankful that today that music is a rich part of their lives.

Later, during our high school years, there were times it would have been helpful to have a tutor or for the boys or to be in a class. When they encountered problems they could not understand and were beyond my ability, I recommended emailing the publishers. That often worked. But I don't think my youngest ever took my advice. I think he was too stubborn and persevered by re-working the problem until he got it. It was my requirement that each wrong answer be corrected, and by their junior and senior years, I allowed them to grade their own work, except for essays.

Despite the bumps along the way, my oldest scored well enough in math on the ACT that he tested out of it for college; however, since he was in the Honors Program, Calculus was required. He earned an A and even tutored other students the next year. My middle son, when he took Calculus in college as part of the Honors Program, said that math was not so difficult when someone explained it to you. In this regard, his high school math was harder than his college Calculus. One time, when in class, his professor said that he had prepared a visual answer to one of the problems but he liked the diagram a student did, better, and up went Eddie's answer for the class to see.

Math had its rough spots, but writing was tough, too, though I very much liked our curriculum, Put That In Writing by Steve and Shari Barrett. Grading essays was my least favorite task. Once when my oldest was in college he called home and asked how I was doing and I said I was crabby because I was grading an essay. He said, "Don't be crabby, just be mean." Being tough with your grades is helpful in the long term.

Chemistry was another subject that gave me trouble, but not the boys. Instead of grading their work with all those confusing significant figures, I let them grade their work themselves. There was dinner to fix, and laundry to do and dogs to walk, and not enough time to get everything done, so that was my solution to my chemistry dilemma. Other subjects my boys studied on their own in their high school years were History, Latin, Greek and Logic.

Though we did not participate in co-ops, my boys were active participants in our local homeschool speech and debate club. Going to tournaments was one of the highlights of their secondary school years. They made friends quickly while learning valuable life skills and were successful as partners with each other and with others. Non-academic activities they participated in included taekwondo, hunting, fishing, trapping, shooting, gardening (selling produce) and work.

With only one year to go with my last son, there are few things I would have done differently. To do all that we did, including reading nearly 500 books aloud before the oldest went to college, going on vacation on our schedule, participating heavily in speech and debate, while at the same time spending money only on books and supplies (and speech and debate), would have made participating in a co-op or online class schedules difficult, though I know many do, and with resulting test scores comparable to my sons. But there are a couple of differences.

Besides the low cost and the scheduling freedom, there is the proof that homeschooling can be successfully done completely in the home, without professionals. It doesn't really take a village; it just takes a family. There is also no doubt that learning independently can be difficult... but not without its rewards. Hebrews 12:1 says: "No discipline seems pleasant at the time, but painful. Later on, however, it produces a harvest of righteousness and peace for those who have been trained by it." Similarly, the discipline of learning on your own, produces a harvest of good character and that good character has its rewards.

Scoring highly on college entrance exams was never the goal. My first son's high scores were a pleasant surprise to me (we never did yearly testing), and very rewarding. With each succeeding son, I wondered if the work accomplished would have the same result. I was thankful when it did. With the scores came scholarships which have helped the older two graduate from college debt free.

None of this would have been possible were it not for those who went before and showed me the way. I stand on their shoulders and reap the harvest of their work, whether it was winning legal battles, or writing curriculum, or paving the path for others to follow. May those who have gone before, our homeschooling veterans, be blessed.

Susan Hoffman is a homeschooling mother and it has been her favorite job, ever. She graduated from Valparaiso University with Distinction and Senior Honors with a BS in Home Economics, did a dietetic internship at the Christ Hospital (Cincinnati) and worked as a staff dietitian B.C. (before children). Being a stay at home mom and looking ahead to schooling options with despair, she rejoiced when she first heard about homeschooling on Focus on the Family. She decided to homeschool all the way through, not "one year at a time". With two graduated and one nearly there, she fills her hours with as many miles on her bike as time and weather allow. Other than that, she has never written to be published and considers it one of her weaker skills.

Memories from a Homeschool Pioneer

Marsena Hatfield

As the school year ended in 1985, I was finishing first grade at a Christian school here in Indiana. There were some problems in the school, so my parents were considering transferring my older brother and me to another Christian school. My mother discussed it with a teacher from the new school, and the teacher suggested my mom homeschool. My mother was immediately overwhelmed and apprehensive. It was the early years of home education and not as accepted as it is today. After much prayer and discussion, my parents took a leap of faith and started the journey of homeschooling. Later, my younger sister joined my brother and me, and we were all homeschooled through high school graduation.

I well remember the spirit of revolution that prevailed in those early years. We were making history! Thankfully we never actually faced persecution, maybe because we had never been to public school, but we lived with the fear that it would come knocking at our door. One day the HSLDA magazine warned us that homeschoolers were receiving phone calls from someone pretending to be a new convert looking for a church and asking personal questions such as, "How do you discipline your children?" My parents were so glad they had been made aware of this because the received a call and were able to answer appropriately. Since we never knew who was on our side, we almost never left the house during school hours, and if someone came to the door that we didn't know, we children hid in the bedroom quietly while our parents answered it. My Mom and Dad attended every IAHE convention and faithfully paid their subscription to HSLDA. If they were asked to call their legislators, they didn't think twice about it, they called. They were fighting for their freedoms!

By the time I was in high school, we didn't think anything about being out during school hours. Homeschooling had become accepted. We went to college without worrying about acceptance based on our school choice. Life had completely changed. We had fought and won.

Time has swiftly passed. I have four children, all of which I've homeschooled, and my oldest went to college this year. I'm sorry to say that at times I've forgotten the sacrifice my parents and others paid for me to be able to teach my children at home. While I'm glad the paralyzing fear of my childhood is past, we need to remember that a price was paid and freedoms must be continually protected. Benjamin Franklin said, "Keep thy shop, and thy shop will keep thee." I'm sure we wouldn't do it an injustice to interpret it to mean that if we guard our freedoms, our freedoms will protect us.

I've recently sensed that the winds of popular opinion are once again blowing, and we as homeschoolers must educate people about the history of home education and continue to fight for what was won in the past. We must be diligent to give our children an adequate education and let our legislators know how we feel. We cannot let what the revolutionaries fought for be in vain. We need to once again remember the reason they homeschooled. It wasn't because it was just an option. It was because they felt "called" to teach their children. It was a conviction. They were determined to keep their children pure and safe, and they also wanted to give them an above average education. In his inaugural address, John F. Kennedy said something about freedom in general that fits how we should feel in the homeschool movement. "We dare not forget today that we are the heirs of that first revolution. Let the word go forth from this time and place, to friend and foe alike, that the torch has been passed to a new generation of Americans, born in this century, tempered by war, disciplined by a hard and bitter peace, proud of our ancient heritage, and unwilling to witness or permit the slow undoing of these human rights to which this nation has always been committed, and to which we are committed today at home and around the world." Let us not forget... freedom is fragile; we must protect it!

Marsena Hatfield is a homeschooling mother of four. She is also a pastor's wife and regional rep for IAHE. She has a passion for ministry and loves to encourage other mothers in their responsibilities.

Hello From The Other Side

Cassie Bottorff

I remember the day that my parents told me they were considering pulling me from the public education system. At the time, I was the tender age of eleven—too young for teenage angst, but old enough to know that something in my life needed to change. I was a bright student, so they said... but the drive that led me to create study guides for my tests led my peers to resent me. The teasing was frustrating enough, but as my parents began investigating the schools that lay before me in the middle and high school years, it became increasingly clear that it was not the environment they wanted me to be raised in. So they took a giant leap of faith, and our homeschool journey began.

I idealized it, at first. No more jeering classmates? Great! I can work at my own pace and finish early? Awesome! School in my pajamas?! YES!! Homeschooling was the best decision ever! But the rose-colored glasses came off quickly, as I came to realize that part of my drive to succeed in school had come from wanting to compete with my peers. Suddenly, the desire to excel had disappeared... and in its place came those glorious teenage years of laziness and contempt.

Oh yes, you know the ones. The ones that say "Why do they make me do this subject anyway? It's pointless! They think I can keep up with all of this AND get my chores done? Dang it mom, I'm a student, not a miracle worker!"

Those were the years that, unbeknownst to me, would set the stage for the rest of my life. I couldn't see it at the time, but things in my life were changing. My curriculum was chosen specifically for me—not for a classroom full of children. My parents were right there to guide me, sometimes with gentle encouragement and sometimes more forceful (which I rightly deserved because, let's face it guys, teenagers need a wake-up call sometimes)... but always in love. And the friends I made turned out to be some of the best people a girl could ever hope to meet. People unfamiliar with homeschooling often say that we're an unsocialized bunch but let me tell you—even in the days before Facebook, texting, and Instagram, we had plenty of social opportunities (and if you've never done a progressive dinner, go organize one NOW. Trust me on this).

By the time my high school years were drawing to a close, I had a much different perspective on things. My parents had become leaders of a local homeschool group, and I had learned a bit about how much effort and sacrifice it takes to pull off a successful homeschooling venture. There were laws, there were a million varieties of curriculum, there were conventions and blogs and teachers of all sorts—and they were all there to help students like me. I was kind of floored when I came to that realization—many of these people were volunteering their time and energy into my friends and myself, and getting nothing in return but watching us grow. I truly hope that we've all made them proud.

Of course, high school is but a mere four years of life, and though it seemed to drag on forever it now seems like a blip in time. College quickly followed suit, and I found myself once again hurled from the comfortable and familiar into the new and different. But this time, I had a foundation underneath me. It was still a Christian "bubble," being a Bible college, yet it brought all sorts of new experiences, and revealed that in many ways I had no idea what I was doing. I believe I changed my major at least three times, and ultimately transferred from that small Bible college to a public university. There, I began to truly see my faith challenged as I was surrounded by students and professors who believed differently than me. There were some definite moments of culture shock, and lots of conversations that led to great friendships. I graduated with my bachelor's degree in 2011, and entered the working world.

What a long, strange trip it's been. I've continued to attend homeschool conventions as an adult, working for various vendors and staying in touch with my "roots." It's become increasingly clear to me over the years that homeschooling is much more than a simple decision to "have school at home." It's a huge lifestyle change, something that sticks with you and—at least in my opinion—positively influences you throughout your life.

Although my husband and I don't have children of our own yet, I'm already amassing lots of books and materials to start their education early. Sure, it'll be a few years before they can read... but I want them to know from the beginning that education starts at home. It may not always be the traditional learning experience, and we might go to gym class in a tae kwon do studio, but we'll make it work. I can only pray that their journey is as rewarding as my own, and that they are eventually as thankful to us as I am to my own parents. I wouldn't be who I am today without the sacrifices that they made. Thanks, mom and dad. What a wonderful journey it's been!

Cassie Bottorff is the eldest daughter of the IAHE's Executive Director, Tara Bentley. She has probably already told you more about her life than you needed to know, but hopefully you enjoyed it. She resides in the foothills of the Appalachian mountains with her husband and two cats, and when she's not sharing her oddball sense of humor with the world she can usually be found curled up with a good book.

Homeschool Helps

Homeschool Helps

The information provided in ***Home Education in Indiana*** is designed to help new homeschool families create a strong foundation. It is not intended to be an exhaustive resource, and we encourage families to continue learning and educating themselves as they endeavor to provide the very best education for their children each year.

The resources included in our Homeschool Helps section are presented for families to have a snapshot of useful information, sample planning tools, and even a sample transcript. These materials represent just a simple snapshot of forms that are useful in quality record keeping.

Attendance Records

IAHE.net

January	February	March	April	May	June	July	August	September	October	November	December
1 New Year's Day	1	1	1	1	1	1	1	1	1	1	1
2	2	2	2	2	2	2	2	2	2	2	2
3	3	3	3	3	3	3	3	3	3	3	3
4	4	4	4	4	4	4 Independence Day	4	4	4	4	4
5	5	5	5	5	5	5	5	5	5	5	5
6	6	6	6	6	6	6	6	6	6	6	6
7	7	7	7	7	7	7	7	7	7	7	7
8	8	8	8	8	8	8	8	8	8	8	8
9	9	9	9	9	9	9	9	9	9	9	9
10	10	10	10	10	10	10	10	10	10	10	10
11	11	11	11	11	11	11	11	11	11 Veterans Day	11	11
12	12	12	12	12	12	12	12	12	12	12	12
13	13	13	13	13	13	13	13	13	13	13	13
14	14	14	14	14	14	14	14	14	14	14	14
15	15	15	15	15	15	15	15	15	15	15	15
16	16	16	16	16	16	16	16	16	16	16	16
17	17	17	17	17	17	17	17	17	17	17	17
18	18	18	18	18	18	18	18	18	18	18	18
19	19	19	19	19	19	19	19	19	19	19	19
20	20	20	20	20	20	20	20	20	20	20	20
21	21	21	21	21	21	21	21	21	21	21	21
22	22	22	22	22	22	22	22	22	22	22	22
23	23	23	23	23	23	23	23	23	23	23	23
24	24	24	24	24	24	24	24	24	24	24	24
25	25	25	25	25	25	25	25	25	25	25	25 Christmas
26	26	26	26	26	26	26	26	26	26	26	26
27	27	27	27	27	27	27	27	27	27	27	27
28	28	28	28	28	28	28	28	28	28	28	28
29	29 (2016, 2020)	29	29	29	29	29	29	29	29	29	29
30		30	30	30	30	30	30	30	30	30	30
31		31		31		31	31		31		31

Sally's Lesson Plans

6th grade: 2016 to 2017

The week of:

	Monday	Tuesday	Wednesday	Thursday	Friday
			Bible for Kids Lesson: _____		
Bible	Day One	Day Two	Day Three	Day Four	Day Five
			Math, one lesson per day		
Math	Lesson:	Lesson:	Lesson:	Lesson:	Lesson:
	Reading:				
Reading					
History	Lesson:	Lesson:	Lesson:	Timeline & Mapping	Quiz
English					
Handwriting					
Geography					
			Practice 30 minutes every day		
Piano					

"To educate a man in mind and not in morals is to educate a menace to society."
Theodore Roosevelt

Field Trip Log

Year:

Location:		Date:	
Activities:			

Location:		Date:	
Activities:			

Location:		Date:	
Activities:			

Location:		Date:	
Activities:			

Location:		Date:	
Activities:			

Location:		Date:	
Activities:			